CONTENTS

DARE TO DIVE IN!

Strategies and Resources for Involving Your Whole Church in Worship

Heather Kirk-Davidoff
Nancy Wood-Lyczak

Abingdon Press
Nashville

DARE TO DIVE IN!
STRATEGIES AND RESOURCES FOR INVOLVING YOUR
WHOLE CHURCH IN WORSHIP

This book is printed on acid-free paper.

Library of Congress Cataloging-in-Publication Data
Kirk-Davidoff, Heather.
   Dave to dive in! : strategies and resources for involving your whole church in worship / Heather
Kirk-Davidoff and Nancy Wood-Lyczak.
      p. cm.
   Includes bibliographical references and index.
   ISBN 0-687-33284-2 (binding: adhesive, pbk. : alk. paper)
   1. Worship programs. I. Lyczak, Nancy Wood.   II. Title.
0
   BV198.K56   2006
264—dc22

                                                                              2005029602

06 07 08 09 10 11 12 13 14 15—10 9 8 7 6 5 4 3 2 1

MANUFACTURED IN THE UNITED STATES OF AMERICA

Acknowledgments

We developed the strategies and resources described in this book through trial and error with the congregations of the First Congregational Church of Somerville, Massachusetts, the First Congregational Church of Claremont, New Hampshire, and The United Church of Winchester, New Hampshire. These congregations taught us what good worship feels like, and we are deeply grateful for the support, love, and care they have given us and our families.

A number of ministerial colleagues gave us helpful suggestions throughout the process of writing this book and the material within it. We are grateful to Greg Morisse, who co-designed the Longest Night Service. We are particularly thankful to Laura Collins, Kipp Gilmore-Clough, Ginny McDaniel, Gayle Murphy, Katie Treadway, and Amy Walter-Peterson, who read full drafts of this book and offered scores of helpful suggestions.

This book would not have been possible were it not for the support of Nathan Lyczak and Dan Kirk-Davidoff, our spouses, and our children, Meg, Rye, Paul, Isaac, and Rosa. As working parents of young children, we were able to make "extra time" in our schedules to write, either separately or together, because our spouses spent even more time caring for kids than they usually do. Nathan and Danny also brainstormed with us, suggested (better) titles, offered gentle critiques, and got us to laugh at ourselves at crucial moments. We are truly blessed to have partners not only in life, but also in many ways, in ministry.

We dedicate this book to them.

WHY DIVE IN?

We believe that God can change people. Do you?

What if worship at our churches was rooted in the conviction that drawing close to God will change our lives? What if members of our congregation began worship each week with the expectation that *something will happen here that will change my life?* How would worship be different?

Heather's Story

My approach to leading worship has changed significantly over the last five years as I've lived more and more fully into my conviction that God can make change in people's lives. For the first five years I was a pastor, I just needed worship to be "good enough." A few weeks before I graduated from divinity school, I was called to be the sole pastor of a small, struggling urban church. My goals were simple: I didn't want to mess up too often or too obviously.

I was content to follow a standard order of worship, each week adding three appropriate hymns from our hymnal and a congregational confession copied from one of my books of worship resources. Since it just about killed me to write a new sermon every week, I had little choice but to run the rest of the worship service on autopilot. But in a way, my understanding of the purpose of worship backed up my approach. I figured that people came to worship to ponder the Big Questions of life. If I could show them a new way to read a piece of scripture, engage them in a challenging idea, or involve them in a story that touched their hearts a bit, I had succeeded. In short, my goal as a worship leader was to have those in attendance say at the end of the service, "Hmm. Good point."

Youth group was a different matter. The neighborhood kids who gathered in the church hall every Sunday night had no interest in being preached at. But they were hungry for anything that could give them hope when they were hopeless, anything that held them when they were afraid, and anything that felt real and true in a world of too much superficiality. Youth group became the place where I talked extemporaneously about my experience of God and prodded and pushed until the kids responded with their own experiences and ideas. I made connections between pop music, movies, comics, and the Christian faith there. I laughed there, often at myself. And I cried there, unselfconsciously and with great relief. My goal, after all, was to make a real difference in the kids' lives, and I was willing to do just about anything if I thought it might take me a step closer to that goal.

About four years into my first pastorate, I went with our youth group to Puerto Rico on a week-long mission trip. It was a transformative experience for many of the kids—and I had a front-row seat to watch the changes that God made in their lives. I saw them take risks they would have never taken back home, reaching out to people who were quite different from them, opening themselves up to each other, and pushing themselves to give more than they thought they had.

One afternoon, we took the kids snorkeling in a secluded cove, something none of us had ever done before. Viewed from the surface, the water looked dark and uninteresting. But once we looked beneath the surface, we were awestruck by the beauty and complexity of coral, fish, and plants. That experience became our metaphor for the whole trip—we went beneath the surface of life, and we witnessed astonishing beauty. When we came back, God wasn't just an abstract idea for the kids. They knew that God has power because they experienced it first-hand.

It was hard to return to the "real world" when we got back. I found myself dissatisfied with much of what I had been doing in the church, especially in worship. I struggled to identify what exactly was bothering me, and finally articulated it this way: my expectations for what could happen in worship had been too low. I didn't just want to make a few good points anymore. I wanted to invite my congregation to go snorkeling—to go beneath the polite surface of greeting and smiling and sharing the news with each other. I wanted to dive down, to experience the beauty and surprise that I knew we would find when we let ourselves go deeper in our relationship with each other and with God.

High Expectations, Low Expectations

When Christian worship began, it was essentially testimony about the power of God to change lives. The early leaders of the Christian church were on fire (literally!) with what they had experienced with Jesus, and later, at Pentecost. They wanted nothing more than to invite everyone they encountered to share that experience with them. They were also aware of how deeply the systems of control and oppression around them were threatened by what they had experienced. But prisons and laws and the scorn of religious authorities could not deter them. They sought only to be authentic witnesses to Jesus' promise of new life.

It's striking—and depressing—to note how much our worship has changed since those early post-Pentecost days. The experience that most mainline church members can expect in worship is highly controlled and predictable. While it is sometimes beautiful, it is based on very low expectations that anything significant will happen as a result of our time together. It is, to be blunt, boring.

The dire condition of worship in many mainline churches became undeniable to me back in 2002 when I (HKD) had a three-month sabbatical from the church I was serving. I looked forward to using this time to worship at churches led by some of my friends who were also clergy. These were engaging, warm, and spirited people, and I was sure that the worship they led would be engaging, warm, and spirited.

Time and again, I was disappointed. I worshiped in half a dozen churches where the experience of being in worship seemed to have a deadening effect on both the clergy and the congregation. As I walked into the church, people would greet me warmly, shake my hand, and often engage me in animated conversation. Once worship began, these same people looked as if they had been shot with a stun gun. Their eyes went blank; their faces went slack. The worship service seemed to drag on, and by the time of the sermon, no amount of theological or scriptural insight could raise the energy level of the congregation.

After worship, the energy of the congregation would pick up again. Coffee hour was filled with chatting, smiling people and shouting kids. I'd accept a cup of tea offered by a cheerful parishioner and begin to socialize; then, within moments, the pastor would pull me aside and talk about her disgust with the congregation and their resistance to change. After telling a few horror stories usually involving her failed attempts to start a new program or eliminate a board, she'd go on to share, in hushed tones, her desire to find a new placement or even a new career, and her sincere doubt about the future of the mainline church.

After about two months of this, I spoke to the denominational executive in charge of my region. "Where should I worship?" I asked him. "Where can I go for worship that's engaging and renewing? What congregation feels alive in worship, like they are really excited to praise God?" He thought long and hard about my question, and finally suggested one church—out of almost one hundred in the area.

We can't accept statistics like that. We must do a better job with worship—not because it will grow our churches or increase our pledges or even save more souls, but because worship that is boring, remote, lifeless, and predictable does not bear witness to the God we have come to know in Jesus Christ. That God is exciting, intimate, life-giving, and surprising—and our worship should be nothing less.

How Do We Get There from Here?

Many worship leaders—lay and ordained—in mainline churches know that something needs to change. Like my pastor friends whom I visited during my sabbatical, they are as bored and discouraged as their congregations, if not more so. But worship remains the sacred cow for many of us. We'll restructure our boards, innovate new educational or outreach programs, change our church sign and letterhead before we change the way we preach, the way we pray, or most of all the way we serve and receive Communion. If we touch those things, we're convinced our congregation will have our heads on a platter.

Conferences on worship tend only to increase our frustration. We sit in massive auditoriums and feel swept away with the music, the lights and sounds, the projection screens, and superstar preachers who make us laugh and cry. But it's impossible to trace a trajectory from the weekly worship at our churches to these awe-inspiring events. The equipment alone costs thousands of dollars, and few people in our congregation have the musical or technological skills that worship of that sort requires. We leave these conferences more discouraged than we were before we came.

But then sometimes, right in the middle of our regular old services in our regular old churches with our regular old folks in the pews, something special happens. Someone makes a prayer request and tells a short story to explain and everyone in the congregation is present and prayerful for a few moments. Or the choir gets it just right. Or the kids show some part of themselves through their art or their music or their laughter that reminds everyone for a moment of the tender blessings of their lives.

These moments happen, often when we're not even trying to make them happen, and they remind us that worship is not just something we make or do or plan. Worship is something we participate in along with the Holy Spirit, the one who St. Paul says prays in us when we do not even know the words to pray.

Those experiences make us want to keep going, because we know that God hasn't given up on our worship even when we have. And because we know that God's going to show up in worship, we want to be there. We are hungry and thirsty for an experience of God that will change us and make us new, each week and every week.

Nancy's Story

About a year and a half into my life as an ordained minister, our congregation decided to start taping our services to appear on the local community access channel. The Catholic Church in town was already doing it, but there was no local Protestant service airing. We decided to give it a try.

The process seemed quite straightforward. Our church paid the fee to become members of the station. Members of our church went to training sessions to learn how to operate the taping equipment. We got our "spot" in the weekly lineup. We told the congregation all about it so that they would be prepared. Then we thought about where best to position the cameraperson in worship so that he could see the altar. We got the camera ready. Then, show time! We taped our first service during a Sunday in Lent, the year that we built the giant, parade-sized puppets and had them to introduce our Prayer of Confession and Assurance of Pardon (see Changed and Challenged by Jesus, page 59).

Here is what we found: we couldn't actually tape the true experience of worship in our church. There was too much movement, too much action, too many voices speaking from many different parts of the sanctuary. A puppet came in from one door. The person playing Jesus walked in from the back of the worship space and sat down occasionally in different pews. Meanwhile, people were speaking from the front of the worship space and others, engaged in worship, were laughing from all different locations around the room.

This frustrated the videographer—he didn't know how to capture all that was happening in worship on film. It inspired me. I began to think about worship as inherently interactive and participatory. It was my husband who first pointed out the fact that, if one could successfully tape every aspect of worship on a given Sunday, then something was very wrong. He was right! To quote the old Nike advertisement, worship "is not a spectator sport." Just like the Christian faith, good worship is incarnational. If people could get as much out of watching a service on TV as they could *being* there in the flesh, then we had better rethink worship altogether.

From trial and error, we did learn to give the cameraperson an outline of the service ahead of time so that he would know where and when action would take place. But even that had to have an element of flexibility and openness, because we really didn't know what was going to happen in worship on any given Sunday. We could and would spend much time in planning, preparation, and prayer, but we also had to be open to the Spirit's movement in our worship.

I didn't always lead worship with dynamic and participatory elements that I knew I was called to create. At times, after a busy week of too many meetings, too many family commitments and too little sleep, I would just stick with the standard format for worship—three hymns, prayers, anthem, sermon—with no element of participation and response in the service. During those times, I would feel the difference in energy and I would know that people could have just stayed home and watched worship on TV. While the cameraperson might have liked those predictable Sundays since things were predictable, it was clear to me that most worshippers could feel the difference and they wanted to be engaged. As one member of our congregation put it, "I can't afford to miss church now. You never know what will happen next." Members of the congregation might watch the service again on TV to remind them of the power of the worship experience, but they wanted to show up and be a part of something that they couldn't get through any other medium than real life.

It was clear that the process of transforming worship started with me as the worship leader. I could believe that worship was simply a matter of transmitting information from one source to another. If so, people could just as easily watch it on TV. Or I could believe that God's transformative power was at work in our worship time and create ways for people to respond to one another and to God. The TV model required less work from me, but live, participatory worship transformed me and changed those around me.

Start by Raising Your Expectations

We believe that you can have powerful, life-changing worship every Sunday no matter where you are, no matter how up-to-date your church's technology is, no matter how cool your parishioners are. The first step to making that happen is simple: you, the worship leader, need to raise your expectations.

The danger in doing this, of course, is that you risk disappointment. And inevitably, you will be disappointed. When that happens, remember that God can change people, and pray that God will come raise your expectations for you since you are having trouble keeping them high by yourself. In our experience, that prayer works.

Then you need to go public with your high expectations. You can begin by talking about the "sacred moments" you have already experienced in worship. Talk about worship at church camp when you were a kid if you have to, but tell stories about what good worship feels like and how it affects you. Encourage others in your congregation to share their own stories—they do have them—and then wonder out loud, "What would it take to have worship like that on a regular basis at our church?" Be clear with everyone that you're not just fantasizing. You believe that life-changing worship is possible, even at your church.

Then Start Making Mistakes

A friend of ours worked as an intern for a large, center city church with very formal worship. Drawing on his background as a jazz pianist, our friend improvised a bit on his children's sermon one Sunday. After worship, the senior minister pulled him aside and said sternly, "At this church, we do things . . . well. Do you understand me?"

If there is anyone at all who has that attitude about your worship service—or if you have that attitude yourself—you need to start your change process there. In order for it to be okay to experiment, it has to be okay to goof up.

We all do it—we misplace our Bible right before the Gospel reading, we announce the wrong hymn, we forget to mention important announcements that someone reminded us of just moments before the service started. We can smooth these little flubs over and pretend they didn't happen, and our congregation may never notice. But we can also turn these mistakes into teaching moments. We can have a little laugh about them with the congregation.

We fondly remember a service we led together where we announced at the start that our youth group was less than a hundred dollars away from its fund-raising goals. As the first hymn began, we looked over our numbers and realized we had added them up incorrectly. We felt obliged to mention, at the conclusion of the hymn, that we had made an error, and that we still needed at least a couple hundred dollars. Sitting down again, Heather found an envelope tucked into her Bible with money that she hadn't counted. We felt obliged to make another announcement, at which point the whole congregation was laughing with us. The lay leader continued worship saying, "While we're awaiting further news of the youth group fund drive, let us join together in the Prayer of Invocation. . . ."

If by some chance you do not actually make mistakes like we do, make one on purpose some Sunday. Don't go overboard—keep your shoes on the right feet and zip up the back of your dress. But don't pretend the mistakes didn't happen. Have a laugh about it. Be sure every single person in your congregation (including you) knows that the roof of the sanctuary will not actually collapse if someone makes a mistake while leading worship. And be sure everyone understands that God does not expect perfection from us. God loves imperfect people.

Claim Three Key Values

Then you're ready to start introducing new elements to your worship service. The kind of worship we are aiming toward is diverse and constantly evolving, but we believe that life-changing worship has some common values:

1. It is participatory. Good worship is never a performance. It is something a congregation does together with God. The worship ideas in this book always reach out to make connections between what is happening up front and what is happening in the pews. Sometimes there is conversation, sometimes there is movement, sometimes the people who usually sit in the pews come up front and lead. But at all times, our goal is to break down the division between worship leader and congregation.

For that matter, the kind of worship we're proposing has points of access for adults, teens, and children. We have intentionally blurred the lines between the parts of the service that are "for the children" and the parts of the service that are "for the adults." All of us benefit when our theological concepts are rooted in story, expressed with vivid images, and connected to experience. And adults, teens, and children grow in faith when they are part of a multi-generational community where they can challenge and encourage each other.

Let's do worship together.

2. It is multisensory. We are interested in making worship more than something you hear. We want to move around more; we want to see more art and movement. We want to touch things—clay and water and bread and each other's hands. We're even open to tasting and smelling good things in worship—anything to get us out of our heads a little bit and into our bodies. Sometimes we need to be confronted with an interesting sense experience in order to give our thinking brains a rest for a moment.

3. It makes use of themes and seasons. We love worship that has a unifying theme, tying together the hymns, the prayers, the sermon, and anything else that happens. But we love even more whole seasons in the church that have a theme. We want our congregations to leave worship each week with a sense of anticipation about what's going to happen next week. And we want to develop ideas and themes that are complex, and one of the best ways to do that is to address them a bit at a time over the course of weeks. We believe in letting things sink in. When we use themes and seasons, one worship service builds upon another, and no one wants to miss the next installment.

Two Words of Warning

1. **Interaction is time-consuming.** If one of your congregation's highest values is for worship to be done within an hour, you will have to shorten or remove some other parts of the service if you make some parts interactive. Better yet, call that value into question by making worship so great that people aren't watching the clock. In this case, we firmly believe it's better to ask for forgiveness than permission.

2. **Interaction doesn't need to happen in smaller groups, but it may need to start there.** While some of the worship ideas in this book are most appropriate for congregations that have fewer than 150 in worship, many of them are useable in congregations that are much larger. But especially if your congregation is large, you may want to begin to experiment with interactive worship in smaller group settings. Give some of these techniques a first run-through at a deacon's retreat, a gathering of small group leaders, an early Sunday service, or your annual family camp.

Ready to Read On?

In what follows, we outline a step-by-step plan for moving your worship out of the predictable routines that have made it predictable and routine, and opening it up to the power of the Holy Spirit. We've introduced these elements in an order that you may find useful: the earlier chapters suggest places to start, while the later chapters suggest directions you can explore once your congregation has begun to get on board with the idea of interactive worship. If your congregation is highly skeptical of change, you will do well to focus your early efforts on beginning worship with short, theme-setting skits (chapter 1) or changing your "children's sermon" into a "Story for All Ages" (chapter 2).

If your congregation is more flexible, or if you've already begun to worship in a more interactive style, you might pick a different starting point. Consider making changes in the sermon time (chapter 3) or in the Confession and Assurance of Pardon (chapter 4). Or introduce some new elements into your Communion service (chapter 5) or suggest changes to the way in which you praise God through music (chapter 6). We have found that special occasions are a great time to introduce new ideas in worship and we have several good resources that span the church year (chapter 7).

Even if your congregation is ready to dive in earlier than most, don't skip the early chapters entirely—they contain plenty to interest even the more "advanced" congregation. What congregation wouldn't be thrilled to have ancient prophets come to their congregation and tell the story of Advent in a new way?

Additional resource material on the CD included in this book supplements many of the chapters. Plus, all the worship resources printed in the book are also on the CD—ready for you to copy and use this week!

One Last Word of Advice

Be open to surprises. Your congregation may be open to things that your never expected them to like. Lay leaders may stand up and say things that touch you at your core. Teenagers may write reflections that show a deeper level of insight than most of your friends in seminary had. And a little old lady may be able to pray in a way that makes the windows shake with the spiritual force of her words.

Be appreciative. Show your delight. But never, ever let on that you didn't think it could happen at your church. Tell them you never expected anything less.

Start the Day with Drama

Surprise!

I (NWL) was due to give birth in a few weeks. It was July. I had just returned a few days earlier from a nine-day youth mission trip to Kentucky (in a van!). The last thing in the world I wanted to do was go to a meeting of the Parish Care Committee.

I considered excusing myself on the grounds that I didn't feel physically up to it. After all, I had just been on a mission trip. Couldn't I get out of a few things just because I was pregnant? Hadn't I done enough? Just as I was going to call to cancel, a member of the committee phoned and offered me a ride, saying how much the committee needed me there. Silently cursing the church and everyone in it, I told her that I'd love a ride to the meeting.

We arrived at the chairperson's house as usual. I opened the door and forty people jumped out at me and shouted, "Surprise!" I had arrived at my baby shower! The house was packed with people of all ages from the church—little kids, youth, working people, and elderly folks—all smiling and laughing at the look on my face.

I was, of course, touched by the congregation's care and generosity toward me. But just as wonderful to me was the transformation of my attitude. I went from resistance and resentment to delight and joy within seconds—all because I had been surprised.

Perhaps you've had a similar experience—a surprise birthday party or an unexpected visit, card, or email from a dear friend. If so, you know the unexpected has the power to transform our mood, our attitude, and our expectations in very powerful ways.

Following God's Lead

The Bible is full of stories of God's breaking into history when people least expect it. Moses meets God in the burning bush. Samuel is awakened in the night by God's voice. Paul falls off his donkey on the road to Damascus as he hears Jesus' voice calling him to a new life. Jesus is born in a stable to two poor and humble young people. It seems that God's *modus operandi* is surprise. Time and again, God interrupts us in our self-absorption and calls us into a new way of thinking, of doing, of being.

If we take the cue from God and bring an element of surprise into our church, we can jump-start the process of transforming worship. Not only does the introduction of something unexpected make us more engaged and excited about worship, it also makes us more open to the Spirit present in our lives. With a small and unexpected addition, we begin to transform our expectations about what is possible in worship. It all begins with how we start the day.

We invite you to start the day with unexpected drama—short skits that "interrupt" what usually happens in worship. These five-minute dramas set the tone for worship, announce the theme of worship for the day, and invite people to playfully invite God into their lives. We start here for a number of reasons:

1. Drama loosens people up.

We know that Protestant churches of the type we lead have been called "God's frozen chosen"—and rightly so. But when we put our toe in the water of worship transformation and added a surprise drama to the standard, formal worship service, our congregations have responded enthusiastically. They smiled and laughed. Those playing parts in the dramas moved about the sanctuary during worship, a first for many. And during coffee hour, people were actually talking about what had happened in worship. Worship and their lives outside the sanctuary were beginning to intersect and they liked it.

2. The Order of Worship does not change permanently.

We know how difficult it can be to make a change in the printed Order of Worship. It can take countless meetings with the deacons or the worship committee to move the anthem up five minutes in the service. The beauty of the unexpected opening drama is that it doesn't mean changing the Order of Worship. By its very nature it is a surprise so it can't even appear in the Order of Worship. So, you don't need to get committee approval!

In addition, surprise elements challenge a congregation's strict adherence to their standard liturgy. I sometimes joke that while my congregation doesn't read the Bible literally, it does read the Order of Worship that way. By adding in something that does not even show up in the Order of Worship, we are modeling that we can be open to the movement of the Spirit. Some things cannot be predicted or planned when we are opening ourselves up to God's power in our lives.

3. You build support as you go.

By definition, in order to have a drama, you have to have actors. When you start the day with drama, transformation in your worship actually starts when you ask people to play a role in the skit you have planned. As soon as people have agreed to participate, they are in on the secret and you can see the enthusiasm and excitement in their faces. The drama becomes very important to them, too. They take ownership of the idea, make suggestions, and start planning. You now have allies in this new venture who are going to help smooth the way in the congregation so that worship transformation becomes everyone's project.

One helpful hint in casting: if you suspect that a more controlling member of your congregation will be upset by not being told about the drama, cast him or her in a part. That way he or she is in on the secret! Rather than complain, we have seen such folks shine in a new role.

4. Don't miss out!

In many churches, if you show up five minutes late for worship, you miss only the announcements that you could have read in the Order of Worship anyway. No wonder people drag in! But when a surprise drama starts off Sunday morning worship, you've got to be there to experience it. With this small change, you have raised people's expectations about what is going to happen in worship and you have set a tone that says, "You've got to be here, on time, or you might miss something."

5. You can't stay here.

After the fifth time you've had an unexpected drama at the beginning of worship it becomes . . . well, expected. By definition, you can't stay at this point forever. Starting the day with drama is meant to be the first step toward worship transformation. It gives everyone a feel for how faithful and fun it is when the whole congregation is involved in worship.

After you have tried out the two opening drama examples included in this book, **Get Moving!,** an Advent drama series found in print and on the CD, and **The Gameboy Can Wait!,** a drama found on the CD that you can use at any time in the church year, you are ready to move further out into the deep end. You'll find that people in your congregation are loosening up and raising their expectations for what worship can be. You'll be ready to try even more ways of being involved in worship that engages the heart, mind, and soul.

Congratulations, you've gotten your feet wet!

Start the Day with Drama:
Get Moving!

Theme: We've got to step out in faith or we might miss God's presence.

Introduction

This opening drama series explores the idea of resistance and stepping out in faith. We believe that there are many reasons why we stay where we are instead of stepping out in faith to engage with God.

- Some of us want more answers. We believe that if we can just find out more about the process, investigate it rationally and weigh all the options, then we'll be ready to go. Of course, we can never be completely ready, so we stay where we are.
- Some of us are afraid of what is new and different. We want security and an airtight plan for how it will all go. Finding no one plan that is 100 percent guaranteed, we opt for the safe and familiar.
- Still others of us adopt an attitude of apathy in order to protect ourselves from the inevitable pain of life. We can't believe that our making a journey of faith will make any difference in the end anyway. Better to conserve our energy and stay right where we are.

In this opening drama series, designed for the four Sundays in Advent, we address those themes head on—with humor and surprise, of course. In the end, all three magi, despite their fears and misgivings, make the trip and report back to us that the risk was worth it. It will be for your congregation as well!

Materials

- 3 magi costumes. These can be as simple as Burger King paper crowns (we know because we've used them) and a bathrobe for each actor. Note that all of the kings will come out together the last Sunday in Advent so you can't use the same costume for each of the three kings (again, we know because we tried).

5

- If you are feeling crafty, consider making the crowns out of big pieces of foam. You can cut out fun and crazy crowns and then decorate them. It's a great youth group activity.

Preparation

- Get costumes together.
- Ask people in your congregation to play the parts. Choose people who you think can comfortably speak in church. Do note that this series involves the actors singing different words to a familiar hymn on the last Sunday. Make sure that you disclose this information to people when you ask them to participate, but singing *well* is in no way a requirement!
- Make sure to have a rehearsal for each play so that people feel comfortable with the role you have given them.

Things to Consider

- This opening drama works best when the magi "interrupt" you as you are opening worship. You will need to tailor the drama to best fit the way you begin worship. We have made suggestions in the dramas themselves for how that might happen, but you will know what is best for your context. Do make sure to practice with the magi the "interruption" so that their entrances make the biggest impact and give the greatest surprise.
- We call them magi for a reason—it is a gender-neutral title. Make sure to invite women as well as men to act in these skits.
- Don't forget the element of surprise. Remind the actors to keep the secret to themselves. Of course, once the second magus has come to worship, people will start to anticipate their interrupting worship. However, at that point, people will begin to wonder, if there are four Sundays in Advent and only three magi, then what will happen on the fourth Sunday.
- This drama series could easily be adapted for use in Epiphany. One by one the magi could interrupt the whole service. (The first magus could come at the beginning of the service; the second after the first hymn; the third following the Assurance of Pardon; and all three could come out together during the sermon.)

Get Moving!
Week 1: I Need to Find Out More

Minister: Happy Advent everyone, and welcome to worship this morning.

(*Proceed through your worship beginning—welcome, announcements, prayer concerns, etc.*)

As today is the first Sunday in Advent, I want to say a little word about that before we begin our worship. This is the time in our church year when we spend four weeks getting ready to celebrate the birth of Jesus on Christmas Day. The fact of the matter is that we've gotten so used to celebrating Christmas Day that we forget that we need to get spiritually ready to welcome Jesus into our lives. We can use these four weeks to step out in faith and discover God in new and different ways.

Our task as a church this Advent is to expect that God is going to urge us forward into a deeper relationship in exciting and new ways. Just as God broke into that stable on Christmas morning, we must believe that God is going to break into our lives in unexpected and life-changing ways. . . .

First Magus: Greetings, everyone! Oh, don't worry about bowing; I'm much too excited to worry about such things.

Minister: Who are you?

First Magus: Can't you tell by my regal clothing? I'm a magus. I have wonderful news to share with you. I have made a very important discovery! There is a very unique celestial presentation right now. . . .

Minister: What do you mean, "celestial presentation"? This is a church, not a PhD seminar in astrophysics.

First Magus: Ahh, I see your point. Well, how shall I put it? You see, what I have observed—I mean, seen—is a . . . a . . .

Minister: A new star.

First Magus: Well, it's definitely new. Since I have studied the heavens nightly since childhood, I'm quite familiar with the usual celestial landscape—that is, the sky—and this is certainly unprecedented—it has never happened before. (*Becoming really excited.*) But as to whether or not it is a star . . . well, to be frank, we're not certain. We have considered the diagnosis of nova or supernova, but it's also possible that we're looking at a comet, although the absence of a plume would suggest otherwise. Some of my colleagues have suggested a planetary convergence, and their interest has been piqued by the fact that this phenomenon is occurring in the constellation Pisces. Intriguing, don't you think?

Oh, I've done it again, haven't I? Sorry, it is just that this, well, for the sake of our conversation let's call it "a star," this star is so exciting to me! I am going to have to study this a great deal more. I am considering, in fact, calling a conference of astronomers from all over the region to come and discuss their findings. Of course, with everyone's schedule, that will take a while to pull together. But perhaps by this time next year we'll be able to convene. . . .

Minister: Wait a minute. What are you talking about? You're going to hold a conference? You're going to have a meeting? Aren't you going to follow the star? Don't you want to go see what's happening over there in the East?

First Magus: Follow the star? Don't be absurd. As I mentioned, we're not even certain that it is a star. You see, a planetary convergence is something else entirely, although a fascinating phenomenon in its own right. How shall I explain it to you? I'd need some paper to show just a few simple equations.

Minister: But haven't you considered that you might have a part to play in God's plan? You can't just spend time studying that star!

First Magus: But studying is what I do. To follow that star without proper planning and forethought would be just plain . . . spontaneous. No, the right course of action is more in-depth analysis.

Minister: Uh, just hold that thought for a minute. (*Aside to the congregation.*) What are we going to do? The magi are a very important part of the Christmas story! What could we do to get him going? (*Brainstorm with the congregation—get their suggestions and respond along these lines.*) Hey, Mr. Magus, we know you have a lot more to study, but could we make a suggestion? We think you should go follow the star, and maybe take some of your friends with you. You could talk together while you're traveling, and we think you'll actually find out a lot more that way.

First Magus: What a novel idea! Sort of a traveling symposium—that means a meeting that moves. Well, yes, I think that could be useful. There is only so much to be learned in a library, after all. And there is something about this star that is so important that it makes me want to step out of my usual routine a bit. Maybe there'll be other people on the road too. Oh, this could really be interesting. I will give it a go, I tell you. And I'll let you know what happens. Thanks for the encouragement!

Minister: I'll bet that our singing would be even more encouragement for our magus friend. Please join me in singing the opening hymn.

Get Moving!
Week 2: I Need a Better Plan

Minister: Welcome to worship on this second Sunday in Advent!
(*Proceed with your usual welcome and announcements.*)
Are there any prayer concerns today?

Second Magus: Excuse me. Sorry to bother you, but I'm looking for a friend of mine. He said something about taking a trip, something about following a star. He said to meet him here, but I think I've missed him.

Minister: Well, we saw him last week, but we haven't seen him today.

Second Magus: Oh, dear, now what should I do? He didn't give me much time to prepare. He was in such a rush, and I just hate that. I don't like to make snap decisions. I like to have a plan. And did that magus have a plan? No. Or at least, not much. I mean, what about a map? What about hotel reservations? Has he considered that? I think not. We've got a huge "to do" list and he just takes off! If you see him, could you tell him that I've gone back home? I've barely started my packing!

Minister: What? You're going back home?? Uh, could you just wait here for a moment? (*Aside to the congregation*) We've got a problem here folks. This magus is an important part of the Christmas story, and it looks like she's not going! We've got to convince her to stop worrying and start moving. Any ideas how we could do that? (*Brainstorm with the congregation and use their suggestions along these lines . . .*) Um, Ms. Magus, we have something we'd like to say to you. We know it's often scary to take a journey when there are so many unknowns, but you know, you won't be alone. There's already one magus out there on the road, and I think there'll be another coming along soon. You all will be in it together, and I know you'll be able to work out some of the details as you go along.

Second Magus: Do you really think so? Did that first magus look like he knew what he was doing? Oh, I suppose you're right. I guess two heads are better than one a lot of times. And that star is so amazing; I really do want to find out what it's all about. Okay, I'll go. I'm not usually so adventurous, but your encouraging words really help. Thanks, everyone! I'll let you know what we find out.

Minister: Well, we certainly have one prayer concern today—for the second Magus to stay on the journey—and for us to as well! Are there other prayer concerns?

(*Proceed with prayer concerns.*)

Get Moving!
Week 3: Who Cares?

Minister: Good morning and welcome to this third Sunday in Advent. As many of you know, we have had unexpected visitors, magi, visiting us at the beginning of worship during this Advent. This Sunday, I'm not even going to try and start worship because I'll bet there is one coming today. I think we should invite the magus to join us by calling out, "Come out, Magus." Will you join me in that? Great. Here goes, "1 . . . 2 . . . 3 . . . Come out, Magus!"

Third Magus: (*Wandering in.*) Hey, dudes, what's all the shouting about?

Minister: Oh, we thought you might be coming today so we thought we would welcome you.

Third Magus: Me? Oh, don't make a big deal out of me. I'm just a magus, man. What's up? Any of you folks know the magi handshake? Kind of goes like this . . . (*Make up something goofy and shake hands with members of the congregation, especially kids.*)

Minister: So, Mr. Magus, haven't you noticed the new star in the East? You should be well on your way toward Bethlehem by now.

Third Magus: Star? Oh, yeah, I think I got a memo about that from another magus. Kind of skimmed it, though. Stars are cool. Yeah. I like to look at them. But man, after a night of star-gazing, I really crash. I gotta sleep in till like noon, or else I'm really dragging during the day. You know what I mean? Matter of fact, I'm thinking of taking a nap right about now. It's been a pretty hectic day already. (*Starts to lie down on the altar.*)

Minister: Hey, don't go to sleep! You got work to do. (*Aside to congregation*) Okay, this guy needs some motivation. We got those other two magi moving, I bet we can help this one out too. What do you think we can tell him that will get him going? (*Brainstorm with the congregation.*) Mr. Magus, we need you to do something very important here. There's something happening in the world, and you need to respond. We need you to travel to Bethlehem. If you hurry, you could probably catch up with two other magi who've gone on ahead of you. They could really use your help and support, and so you really need to go. NOW!

Third Magus: Well, okay, if you really feel strongly about it, I guess I could go. But I'll need to rest up before a big trip like that....

Minister: No.... NOW! Come on, everyone, say it with me. NOW!

Third Magus: Hey, man, I can really feel your energy. That's cool! Okay, Bethlehem, here I go. Wait up, other magi dude and dudette!!

Minister: I really feel the energy, too. Let us continue with our worship now . . .

Get Moving!
Week Four: We're Moving!

(This time have the Magi enter as soon as the Prelude is over.)

Magus 1: Well, my friends, we're almost to Bethlehem and that star continues to be the brightest one in the sky. Do you think it is a supernova? What do you think of my theory of a planetary convergence?

Magus 3: Dude, what are you talking about?

Magus 2: All I can say is I'm so glad this journey is almost over. I can't wait to get to Bethlehem and take a nice hot shower at the Inn.

Magus 1: Sorry, my dear, but showers haven't been invented yet.

Magus 2: Oh, you're right. Well, at least I'm glad that I thought to send a carrier pigeon ahead to the inn so that we would have reservations. Not having reservations stresses me out! I always worry about whether it will be all filled before we get there.

Magus 3: You need to learn to relax. I mean, can you imagine that there'd really be no room at the inn? We're talking Bethlehem here. There's like a bazillion hotels around here.

Magus 1: I feel like I've learned a lot on this journey. And not just about stars.

Magus 2: Me, too.

Magus 3: Hey, you guys, let's sing that song we wrote a couple of days ago.

Magus 2: You mean the Syrian Swing?

Magus 1: The Judean Jitterbug?

Magus 3: No, I was thinking about the one we wrote in the sandstorm. Remember?

Magi 1 and 2: O, yeah. Let's sing it!

(*To the tune of "We Three Kings"*)

Magus 1:
I'm the one who's a bit of a geek.
I've studied the stars for a year and a week.
But I needed a prod
To find out about God,
I know I shall find what I seek.

Magus 2:
I'm the one who hates to leave home.
Without a clear plan, I never would roam.
But thanks to your prod,
I'm off to find God,
I no longer moan and groan.

Magus 3:
I'm the one who couldn't care less.
I'd rather do nothing than deal with the stress.
You gave me a prod
To find out about God,
And wow, dude, my life you have blessed.

All:
What would it take to get you moving too?
Too smart? Too worried? You don't have a clue?
Do you need a prod
To find out about God?
You'll find that the world is made new!
(*Magi gesture to invite whole congregation to sing.*)

Whole Congregation:
"Oh . . . Oh. . . . Star of Wonder . . ."

Minister: What a great way to start worship on this fourth Sunday in
Advent! Let's give our magi friends a round of applause! A good chorus
of "We Three Kings" always starts worship off right . . .

Story for All Ages

It Can Be Better Than This!

We have our share of children's sermon horror stories. You probably do too. Here's an extreme example.

A few years ago I (NWL) went to a new church for the four o'clock Christmas Eve service, my five-year-old daughter in tow. The pastor announced the children's sermon in this way. "Right now, I am going to give all the parents here tonight a special Christmas gift—ten minutes without your children." Uh oh, I thought, this is not an auspicious beginning. It just went downhill from there. The pastor had the children sit on the floor at his feet while he remained in his throne-like chair; he literally talked down to them. His message had to do with the way in which God talks to us. He asked the children questions, and it was clear that there were right and wrong answers. He had the truth. It was the children's job to guess it. At one point a child asked, "Why is it that God sometimes speaks to us in a quiet way?" Good question, I thought. The pastor answered the child with a voice full of certainty. Then he looked up and out at all the parents present and said, "The truth is that I can say whatever I want, and they have to believe it." It was all I could do at this point not to run up to the altar, grab all the children, and yell, "Run for it. Close your ears and run away from this man as fast as you can!"

It is easy to see the speck of dust in another's eye (okay, in that pastor's case it was a telephone pole) and not see the stick in our own eye. We'll admit that we've made plenty of Story for All Ages blunders in the past:

forgotten key props, forgotten well-known children's names, etc. But we have learned from them. We have come to see the power that good storytelling, communal creative inquiry, humor, and humility have for people of all ages.

New Name for a New Concept in Worship

But wait. No doubt you have noticed the phrase "Story for All Ages" in the preceding paragraphs. You may be thinking, "What do they mean by 'Story for All Ages'? Didn't they mean the 'children's sermon' or the 'children's story'?"

We use the term "Story for All Ages" intentionally. In most churches there is a time in the service when the children are invited to come forward and the pastor or another adult delivers a short message to them on themes of being loving, or being thoughtful. It is a time strictly for the kids, and the message is geared for the preschool and early grade school set. By contrast, the Story for All Ages time is for everyone. It is not the sermon "lite" time, and it isn't just for kids. The Story for All Ages time is for everyone to engage playfully in the theme of worship for the day and to bring their whole selves in worship.

We are used to responding to God in church in a few socially acceptable ways—we sing, we pray, we listen, and some of us talk. In many churches, that is about the gamut of options available for engaging in worship. All of those are fine ways to connect to God. They're just not the only ways.

The Story for All Ages time allows people to play, to laugh, and to move their bodies in worship. When creativity and faith combine, you can provide people with the opportunity to expand their understanding of what worship can be and to see that church, at its best, is a whole-body experience. And we need that. We need to feel the affirmation to others when we find the hidden clue and people clap. We need to pray the Lord's Prayer with whole-body gestures and feel the power of praying with our arms and legs, not just our heads. We need to laugh with ourselves and see that the Christian life is not about taking ourselves too seriously. We need to draw and model with clay and thumb wrestle in worship. Because, when we get into that playful spirit, we are more likely to stop listening to the judging, analyzing voices in our heads and just BE in God's presence. Like when we get down on the floor and have a tickle festival with our children, we give our minds a rest and, through play, can joyfully be in the moment. In those joyful, playful moments our whole beings say "Yes!" to God.

This isn't tinkering with your children's sermon time. This is adding a new element to the worship life of your church—a time when imagination, creativity, and whole-body activity are used to engage people of all ages in the worship theme.

Why Do This Next?

By replacing the children's sermon with a Story for All Ages time you have an excellent chance of successfully implementing a lasting and important change into your congregation's worship life. The beauty of this strategy is that you probably already have time in your worship service for the children's sermon so you don't have to add something new to the Order of Worship. While it appears that you have just changed the name of that time you spend with kids in worship, what you have really done is to expand the adults' understanding of how engaging and meaningful worship of God can be. And you have introduced a worship experience that honors creativity, that welcomes spontaneity, that engages our senses, that allows us all to take ourselves less seriously, and that takes God's power very seriously.

"It's for the Children"

When we let our imaginations run wild, we dream of what worship could be like. When we read scripture and pray, we see visions of how we can creatively help people connect more fully to God's infinite love in worship. But, before we can implement these visions and dreams, we self-edit, fearing the discouraging voices in our congregations who tell us such change isn't possible or welcome in our particular context for ministry. We all have people in our congregations who resist new ideas and we fear that the work of trying to persuade them to try out the change requires more energy than we have.

But there is hope. Just use the excuse, "It is for the children." Nine times out of ten, folks who feel resistant to a new idea are going to say, "Well, if 'it's for the children' I guess we can give it a try." It is a great tactical starting point because the resistance will be lower and people will be willing to cut you slack when it is "for the kids." And, the beauty of ideas that are truly gifts of the Spirit is that once people begin to interact with the new ideas, one another, and God, they can't help but want to do so all the time. Creativity in the Story for All Ages time gets you out of the starting block and diving into the pool.

Here is a list of some of the things that we have been able to do in worship during the Story for All Ages time.

- Everyone in the congregation finds a partner and thumb wrestles.
- The whole congregation joins hands and then passes energy from hand to hand all the way around the sanctuary.
- All the children and youth in the congregation, blindfolded, make animal noises to find one another while all the adults cheer them on and make sure that they don't get a concussion by running into the baptismal font.
- Bible Betty, that famous talk show Diva, makes her appearance in the congregation to tape an episode of her award-winning show "As the Bible Opens." (You should have seen her outfit!)

Now, if we had gone to our deacons with many of these ideas we probably wouldn't have gotten very far. We would have been told that worship is not a place for such activities. However, since they were introduced in the Story for All Ages time, and it was "for the children," people entered into the action with an openness and sense of humor that they probably would not have had during the sermon time.

But please note, while the excuse that it's "for the children" works and it is true that children will be engaged by your creativity, never forget that the Story for All Ages time is really for everyone, and plan and dream accordingly. While adults may be most convinced by the rationale that some change in worship is "for the children," it is often they who are most touched by the energy and spirit of the Story for All Ages time.

Age Appropriate to Everyone

We fully recognize that by changing from the children's sermon to the Story for All Ages in worship we no longer gear everything during this time to children. Certainly children are welcomed and respected in this time and find the activity and the sensory stimulation exciting and meaningful. But this isn't only for them. In fact, some of the examples we have included contain theology and humor that is not age appropriate for preschoolers. That's okay. Different parts of each Story for All Ages time will speak to different age groups but all will be engaged in their own way. And, you may be surprised by what concept brings meaning to which age group of people.

During Lenten worship one year our congregation explored stories from the Book of Exodus. An artist in the congregation created large black and white posters of the Exodus scenes, and these formed the foundation for our Story for All Ages time. I knew that the adults and teens were engaged in what we were doing. I wasn't so sure about the young kids.

At Easter vigil, the youth group painted the black and white posters with vibrant watercolor and hung them up in the sanctuary for Easter morning to announce the Resurrection. When we came to the Story for All Ages time, before I could begin speaking, my son shouted out, "Mama, look! That's the picture of the water coming out of the rock and now it is in color!" I know he didn't get the theology behind the Exodus pattern of captivity, wilderness, and Promised Land like the teens and the adults did that year, but he had learned a Bible story that had touched his life. We have to trust that when we tell Stories for All Ages with honesty, respect, and faithfulness, God gets the message needed to everyone in the ways they need to hear it.

Will It Be Hard?

Well, yes and no. It will be easier than you think to get the people in your congregation excited about the energy and action happening during the Story for All Ages time. We believe that people innately want church to be engaging and transforming. If you embark on enlivening your Story for All Ages time, people are going to naturally follow your lead.

That said, some of this will be harder. We're going to level with you: it takes more effort to make happen one of the Story for All Ages series we describe in this chapter than it does to, say, take an item out of a paper bag and talk about it. The hassle factor goes up as the engagement quality of the material you use goes up.

But you don't have to do it alone. Use these Story for All Ages series as an opportunity to invite people into the process of preparation for worship. Match people's gifts and skills with the work that you have to do and then get everyone together for an evening and do it. This is helpful in two ways. First, you can get your entire Story for All Ages preparation done in one intensive session. Then you can breathe more easily for the rest of Lent or Advent or whatever liturgical season you are in. Second, and more important, when you invite people to become a part of the creative process, they take ownership in it. The people who helped you make puppets or helped you sew costumes or who agreed to play a part in a skit are going to be your ambassadors for change to your congregation. They are going to catch the Spirit too and will share their excitement with others they know. While you will be supported in the planning and execution of the production of these Story for All Ages series, you will also build support for your overall vision of the church as a place where energy, engagement, and transformation are the norm.

What If There Are No Kids This Sunday?

Jesus said when two or more are gathered he is with us. We think the same is true for the Story for All Ages —if you have two people in worship, you can have a great time. No matter whether there are one hundred kids or no kids on a Sunday morning, when you are doing a Story for All Ages the show goes on. Remember, this is for everyone.

We think that the Story for All Ages concept is particularly well suited for small congregations with small Sunday schools. In such congregations the kids who do attend worship tend to be constantly on the spot during the children's sermon. They have to answer all the questions and always be the center of attention. With the Story for All Ages time, everyone is engaged and participating, no matter what their age, and it takes some of the pressure off the young people.

Announce the Theme

We encourage you to think about the Story for All Ages time in your worship service as the vehicle through which you introduce the theme for worship that Sunday. In the span of five or ten minutes, you thoughtfully and creatively announce to all present what worship is going to be about this Sunday. Think of this time as the door handle that you make available to people so that they can grasp what corporate worship will be about and open themselves up to God and enter into full Communion with God.

Scripts

We've included three Story for All Ages examples for you to use in your congregations. In print and on the CD you will find **Making Room** and **Not Just for Prophets,** two Advent Story for All Ages series. On the CD we've included **Hide and Seek with God,** designed for use at Lent. Once you have selected a Story for All Ages series and printed it out, next comes the question of how to use scripts in worship.

Here is how we do it. We always use scripts when other people are a part of the Story for All Ages time and we never do when we are the only ones giving the story. We think that it is just too much to ask for other people to dress up in costume and perform in worship and have to memorize their part. Also, if they aren't 100 percent sure of their lines, they might start improvising and go in a direction that we don't want them to go in. We have found it best to give people parts and to rehearse with them but to have them use their scripts in worship.

When we are doing the Story for All Ages time alone, we never use scripts. This style of interacting with people feels most natural and comfortable to us. However, you need to find a style that works best for you. You could jot down a few ideas on a note card or use an outline if that is going to make you most comfortable. The point here is to interact with the congregation in a way that is authentic and that engages everyone.

Amplification

Make sure that everyone in the congregation can hear what is being said. Always use microphones and encourage everyone involved to speak succinctly and slowly.

Remember those folks who were the most skeptical about change in worship? They are going to be fully engaged in the Story for All Ages time and will be hanging on every word that gets spoken. Make sure that they can hear and experience it all!

Making Room: Advent Series

Theme: We have to make room so God can come into our lives.

Introduction

For most of us, the preparation for Christmas involves adding things in our lives—attending Christmas parties and concerts, baking Christmas cookies and shopping for Christmas presents, writing Christmas cards and thank you notes. We go through the season of Advent in a whirlwind of activity, trying to squeeze more and more activities into our already busy lives.

This series playfully invites us to examine what we might have to let go of and how we might have to change in order to make room for Jesus in our lives. Like the cow in the stable, the stars in the sky, and even the expectant holy parents, we have a role to play in God's drama and often that role involves making room for God's spirit to move in our lives.

Materials Needed

- Cow costume. You can use a homemade costume (construction paper spots and ears) or buy one. Don't forget to ask around. You'd be surprised who has a cow costume in his or her closet!
- Star costumes. All you need for these costumes is cardboard and aluminum foil. Cut out five stars large enough for actors to wear on their faces. Cut out face holes and cover with aluminum foil. Attach string so that actors can wear the stars.
- Fun costumes. For week 3, you will need three or four people willing to put on fun, flamboyant costumes as if they were going to do the Story for All Ages for the week. This is a great time to raid your kids' dress-up box.
- Christmas Nativity Play costumes. You'll need biblical garb for the people playing the Inn Keeper, Mary, and Joseph. Most churches have a box of such costumes in a closet. If yours doesn't, bathrobes and a few long scarves can be easily transformed into perfectly adequate costumes.

Preparation

- Get costumes together. If you are going to have to make some, invite others from your congregation to participate in the construction. Be sure to keep the content of the series a secret so that everyone can be surprised and excited about Advent worship.
- Ask a variety of people in your congregation to play the parts for the Advent Series. Choose people who you think can comfortably speak in church. Allow people who are often seen in one role (serious, strict) to cultivate another part of themselves. While this series is written with adults in mind, consider an intergenerational cast. For example, in the "star" play, it is very effective to have a child play the new star role.
- Make sure to have a rehearsal for each play so that people feel comfortable with the role you have given them.
- Talk up the special things that will be happening in worship during Advent. For example, write a newsletter article in which you entice people with the statement, "We are going to have some rather unexpected and uncommon visitors in church during Advent. Don't miss it!"

Things to Consider

- Preach on the theme of "making room" for Advent.
- In many churches, children participate in the Story for All Ages time and then are sent out to Sunday school with a congregational song. For this series, sing a refrain from favorite Christmas carols to conclude each time. We have made suggestions for each week but you may want to choose your own.
- Have a "clean out your closet day" during Advent. Have people survey all their stuff and decide what they need to clean out in order to make room for Jesus in their lives.
- Many churches light an Advent wreath for the Sundays in Advent. Consider having the characters in the "Making Room" series light the candles during the singing of the hymn at the end of each time.

Making Room
Advent Week 1: Making Room in the Stable

Inn Keeper: Hi, cow. I'm going to have to ask you to move from your stall for a few days.

Cow: Moooooove?!!

IK: Yes, you see, I'm in a bit of a bind. I've got this very nice young couple—she's about to have a baby any minute, a very special baby, I am told—and they need a place to stay and I'm full at the house. What do you say, can you make room for them by moving over a few stalls?

Cow: Moooooove! Moooove! Mooove! Why do I always have to moooove? Why don't you ever ask the donkey? He never has to moooooove!

IK: Come on, cow! You know how it is when tax registration season comes around. I haven't a spare bed in the house. And you've got that nice bed of straw, much better than the donkey's. I figure if the baby comes while they're here, they could put him in your manger. What do you say?

Cow: A baby in my manger! Do you know what babies do? They eat, sleep and, well . . . you know! Do you think I want that in my manger? I eat out of that!

IK: I know I'm asking a lot of you. But I am told this is no ordinary baby, and even if it were, sometimes we gain the most when we are asked to do things that make us a bit uncomfortable. (*Becoming more expressive.*) Sometimes, when we are pushed out of what is familiar, we are able to grow in new and exciting ways. Sometimes, when we make room for something new, we enlarge our understanding of the world. Sometimes, that's when we discover the greatest lessons. That's when we learn more about God. (*Declaring loudly with a big gesture.*) It is in making room, my bovine friend, that we find Hope!

Cow: Okay, Inn Keeper, I am willing to moooove in with the donkey and make roooooooom for this family. I'll admit, I'm intrigued about the special baby part. But I'll do it on one condition.

IK: What's that?

Cow: No moooooooooooore of your little mini-sermons.

IK: Deal! I'll leave that for the baby when he grows up. I'll bet he'll give some great sermons. Let's ask the kids to sing a song with us. How about "Away in a Manger"?

All: (*Singing*) "Away in a manger, no crib for a bed..."

Making Room
Advent Week 2: Making Room in the Sky

Star #1: Okay, it's show time! Just about dusk . . . time for the stars to SHINE!

Star #2: What's our opening number tonight? (*Singing*) "When you wish upon a star . . ."

Star #3: (*Singing*) "You . . . light up my life . . ."

Star #4: No, it's (*singing*) "You must be my lucky star 'cause you make the darkness seem so far . . ."

#1: Let's stick with a classic: "Twinkle, twinkle little star."

#3: I hate that song! I refuse to perform it! It completely violates my sense of artistic integrity!

#4: Well then, fine, don't perform it. I'll do the whole thing as a solo!

#1: Wait a minute, we work as an ensemble here. Now all of you fall into place. Behind me!

#2: Why do you always lead our entrance? I can out-twinkle you any day!

#1: Oh, yeah? Watch this! Ladies and Gentlemen, be prepared to be dazzled! (*Singing, dancing*) "Twinkle, twinkle . . ."

New star: (*Entering, bumping into everyone*) Umm, excuse me. Pardon me. I have to get through here.

All the others: (*Talking at once, upset*) Who the heck are you? Can't you see we're in the middle of a number here?

New star: Oh, I'm so terribly sorry to interrupt. But my instructions are quite clear. I need to shine right here, directly over this stable in Bethlehem.

#3: I can't take this! I refuse to perform under these conditions!

#4: This is definitely a contract violation!

#1: Look, kid, you can't just go barging in here, shining wherever the heck you feel like it. We've got a constellation going here, and you're going to confuse a lot of people if you just suddenly appear in the middle of it. Who knows what kind of meaning they'd read into that.

New star: No, my instructions are quite clear. And believe me, I have this from the HIGHEST authority.

#2: (*Unscrolling a large piece of paper*) Well, would you look at that! Here it is in the fine print of the contract. "Arrangement of constellation subject to divine intervention." I'll be! That's never happened before!

#3: Oh ... um ... I guess we will have to move!

#4: I guess we are going to get rearranged!

#1: Okay, guys, let's see if we can make this work out. What are we performing anyways?

New star: (*Singing*) "O star of wonder, star of light, star with royal beauty bright, . . ." (*Everyone joins in*)

Making Room
Advent Week 3: Making Room in Our Worship Service

Worship Leader #1: I was going to invite the children up for the Story for All Ages, but we've got a lot going on in this service, so I think we'll have to skip it today.

Worship Leader #2: But we always do a Story for All Ages! People are counting on it. We've got people in costumes and scripts . . . everyone's been practicing. What are you going to tell them?

People in Costume: (*Entering*) Yeah. We've been practicing for days and just check out our finery!

Worship Leader #1: Well, maybe they can do it another time. But we've got a really full service. We just don't have room. . . .

People in Costume: (*Going back to their seats, grumbling and saying things like . . .*) Well, see if I ever participate in church again! And I got out of bed for this! Man, this was gonna be my big break.

Worship Leader #1: Okay, moving right along. Hmmm, now that I look at it, we're going to have to cut some of that music too. (*Addressing the Music Leader*) If you don't mind, we're just going to skip over the offertory piece you were going to do, and maybe nix the final hymn too. We'll just go straight to the postlude, okay?

Music Leader: Well, I don't know. We've been rehearsing that piece all week, and it's one of my favorites.

Worship Leader #1: I'm sorry, you're just going to have to be flexible. After all, that's what our story series has been about for the past couple of weeks, right? You've got to be flexible and make room if you want God to come into your life! Which reminds me, we're going to have to cut the choir anthem as well. You guys really have sung enough already.

Choir: Aww, man! That was a great song!

Worship Leader #1: Well, let's go straight to the prayer. (*Addressing the person who leads the prayers*) If you don't mind, could you keep it kind of short? Maybe we could skip prayer requests this week—I mean, I know we all have stuff to pray about; but this week, due to time constraints, I think we should just . . . pray silently. Well, actually if that's what we're going to do, we might as well pass the offering while we do it and get that out of the way. Hey! This really is a quick way to worship! With any luck, we can still have a fifteen-minute sermon AND we'll get out of here fifteen minutes early! We should do this every week! This is much more efficient!

Everyone: Wait a minute! That's not the point!

Worship Leader #1: Huh? I thought you guys like to get out of here on time!

Someone in the choir: Well, that's true. Sometimes we do get antsy! But the truth is, we've come here to worship, and we don't want to hurry about it. We want to take the time—make the room—to let our hearts open up to God.

Prayer Leader: In prayer!

Music Leader: In music!

Choir: In song!

Worship Leader #2: And in story! But now that we've said all of this, I guess we don't really need a Story for All Ages after all.

Worship Leader #1: You know, this Sunday all of you really preached to me! Thank goodness for the ways God moves in our lives. Let's all sing, "O Come, O Come, Emmanuel."

All: (*Singing*) "O Come, O Come, Emmanuel, . . ."

Making Room
Advent Week 4: Making Room in Our Lives

Joseph: Okay, Mary, let's get back on that donkey. Only another day's travel and we should be in Bethlehem. Listen, could you do me a favor and hold this water jug on your lap while we go the next leg here? Oh, wait a minute. You don't have a lap anymore, do you?

Mary: No lap, and not much of a stomach either. You know, I was starving when we stopped, but just a few bites of bread and I'm sick with heartburn! This baby's pushed my stomach just about back up my throat! I can even feel him pressing on my lungs, and it feels like I can't really take a deep breath! He better be born soon, because I don't think there's much more room inside of me for him to grow any bigger!

Joseph: Well, you know, your guts aren't the only thing that this guy's gonna rearrange.

Mary: Oh, I know, I know!

Joseph: Yeah, for one thing, there's our spring vacation plans. You know my folks' condo down on the Galilee is adults only, so I guess we won't be visiting them. And I guess we won't be doing a lot of hang-gliding or parasailing, either.

Mary: I didn't realize that's what you had planned!

Joseph: Well, I don't know if I did. But I could've, that's the thing. And that little two-seater convertible sports . . . chariot I've always dreamed of. I guess that's pushed clear out of the picture too.

Mary: Well, it's true that we're all going to have to rethink our plans now that this baby's going to be born. But I think we're going to find it a whole lot easier to make room for him once he's here among us and we can really know and love him.

Joseph: What do you mean?

Mary: I don't know . . . it just seems like a lot of times we don't know how to make room for things we don't understand. Our own plans and dreams seem so much more vivid and immediate than some kind of undefined promise for the future. But a baby has a way of taking over your life. I've seen it before—just look at my cousin Elizabeth! Somehow, once he comes, once we meet him face to face, I just have a feeling that all the other things we think are so important now will suddenly seem a lot less important. We don't really know what we're in for, but I have a feeling that if we just let ourselves fall in love with this baby, we'll find there's plenty of room in our lives for him.

Joseph: Okay, but I'm not moving out of Nazareth! After this trip, my traveling days are over!

Mary: We'll see about that. In the meantime, let's sing on our journey. How about "O Little Town of Bethlehem"?

All: (*Singing*) "O little town of Bethlehem..."

Not Just for Prophets
Advent Story for All Ages Series

Theme: Connecting prophetic wisdom with the birth of Christ urges our congregations to consider how they might actively engage with Jesus in their lives.

Introduction

This Advent series emphasizes spontaneity and excitement. The people of your congregation will joyfully anticipate worship because they expect someone exciting to show up. Worshipers will be abuzz with questions of "Who?!" and "When?!"

More than just excitement will grab people's attention. As they engage with these prophets, folks in your congregation will make connections between the Hebrew Scriptures, the story of Jesus' birth, and their own lives. By laughing with one another, they will come to see how they are a part of God's drama. They will also be compelled by the message the prophets bring. Through this series, worshipers will come to see the different ways prophets spread the news to "get ready." From calling us to accountability to cheering us on, from telling us to clean up our lives to leading us forward on a journey to wholeness, we come to see the variety of prophetic wisdom, and take it to heart in our own lives.

If you preach by the Common Lectionary, you will note that this series corresponds with the Hebrew Scripture readings for Year C. But we believe you can use it any year!

Materials Needed

- Costumes for the four prophets. Jeremiah is a lawyer and could dress in a suit and carry a briefcase. Malachi is a janitor and could be dressed in jeans and a T-shirt or work overalls. Pom-poms and a cheerleader outfit are a must for Zephaniah. Micah, the hiker, should be dressed in hiking gear—backpack, hiking boots, bandana, sun hat.

- Minimal props. Jeremiah needs a briefcase, cell phone, and envelope with the "verdict" inside; Malachi needs a box of Fullers' soap (decorate a laundry detergent box with the words "Fullers' Soap") and a push broom; Micah needs a Bible.

Preparation

- Get costumes together. If you are going to have to make some, invite others from your congregation to participate in the construction. Be sure to keep the content of the series a secret so that everyone can be surprised and excited about Advent worship.
- Ask people in your congregation to play the parts for the Advent series. Choose people who you think can comfortably speak in church. Consider having fun with the genders of the prophets. For example, how would it play in your congregation for Zephaniah, the cheerleader, to be a man? Have fun with your casting.
- Make sure to have a rehearsal for each monologue so that people feel comfortable with the role you have given them.

Things to Consider

- Tailor these monologues to meet the needs of your worship team. You will see that Malachi calls the minister "Lady" in his monologue. That is because the two people who wrote these are women! Perhaps he (or she) might call you "bud" or "man" or "guy." Use your congregational context and adjust the language as needed.
- The element of surprise is important in this series. You as worship leader should have some sort of little mini-Story for All Ages planned that the prophets can barge in on. Many churches light an Advent wreath this time of year. If that is part of your tradition (or if you want to make it a tradition), begin the Story for All Ages time by inviting the young people to participate in the lighting of the Advent wreath. As you are wrapping that up and it appears that your time together is ending, the prophets can barge in on you. Just make sure that you and the prophets have practiced your timing so that it all feels exciting and spontaneous.

Not Just for Prophets
Jeremiah: Prosecuting Attorney

Pardon me, excuse me, apologies to all assembled for my tardy entrance. (*Hands business card to minister.*) Yes, my name's Jeremiah. That's Jeremiah, Esquire, actually . . . and I'll take it from here.

I've been called this morning to read to you the indictment in the case of the Lord God versus the people. There are some fairly serious charges filed here, but I'll try to be brief.

(*Reading paper*) Let's see . . . article one . . . actions in violation of the covenant. Subpoint A, worshiping other gods . . . subpoint B, worshiping still other gods . . . subpoint C, worshiping lots of things that aren't really God at all. (*Looking up from papers*) Wow, that's bad. You folks must not have read the fine print of the covenant. It says right here—"you shall worship no other gods before me." That means that all the other priorities in your life have to take a backseat to your faithfulness to God.

But I didn't come here to counsel you all. I'm here to indict you! You know what that means—you're going to have to go see the judge about what you've done. And the consequences of this kind of behavior are pretty clear. (*Reading papers*) Cities laid to waste . . . no more rain . . . crops dying . . . overtaken by foreign powers . . . led into captivity . . . Nope, not a lot of good news here. (*Scanning crowd.*) Sorry to be the one with the bad news, but I'm just doing my job. (*Begins to pack up briefcase . . .*)

Excuse me. I'm expecting a call. (*Answers his cell phone.*) What's that, Your Honor? (*Whispers to the audience*) Most important call. It is God on the line. (*Into the phone*) Yes. I'm right here. Your final verdict? Well, I guess I could read that too, Your Honor, but I think I've depressed these people enough already. What's it going to come down to—capital punishment? How about hard labor? I might actually recommend that. More productive—get these people out digging some ditches or something.

Oh, okay, I'll read your final sentence to them. (*Opens up briefcase, takes out an envelope and unfolds the letter inside.*) Let's see here . . . Judah saved . . . Jerusalem to live in safety . . . area of habitation will hereafter be entitled, "The Lord is our righteousness." What?!! You intend to pardon these people?! After all they've done??

I just don't understand it. Clearly, your Honor, you've got a different sense of justice than the rest of us do. (*Hangs up cell phone. Slams briefcase shut and starts walking out, shaking his head and muttering.*) Quite extraordinary . . . I guess I'd better do some review of the precedents . . . The next thing you know, God is going to send them a Messiah!

Not Just for Prophets
Malachi: Janitor

Minister: Well, that concludes our Story for All Ages time . . .

Malachi: Excuse me. You gotta move. Got some cleaning to do and you're in the way.

Minister: Don't tell me, you're a prophet, too.

Malachi: Malachi. Janitorial Service. Our motto: we'll get out your spiritual grime before judgment time.

Minister: Sounds pricey.

Malachi: Oh no. We're a not-for-profit prophet cleaning business.

Minister: Yes, but we've already been visited by the prophet Jeremiah, last week. And, to tell you the truth, you all can be kind of harsh.

Malachi: Harsh. I'll tell you what's harsh, this place is harsh. You got a real dirty disaster here. You got sin and hatred everywhere. (*Inspecting the lectern*) Just as I thought, shoddiness and sloppiness all over. (*Moves to the pulpit and runs a finger across the surface.*) Corruption and desecration buildup! I haven't seen a pit like this since Ancient Edom.

Minister: "Corruption, desecration, Ancient Edom"? You're in the wrong century, Mal, maybe the wrong millennium. Next thing you know, you're going to tell us we're offering the wrong kinds of animals for sacrifice.

Malachi: Lady, we prophets aren't just about animal sacrifices anymore. We show up when we see that folks need some help in seeing themselves and God clearly. You could say that we scrub your windows clean so you can see out of them clearly. . . . Speakin' of scrubbing, this place needs a major overhaul. I'm gonna give you my super "Righteousness Cleaning."

Minister: I'm sorry, but shouldn't we check with the trustees first? I mean, we didn't vote on this.

Malachi: No time, lady. Got my orders. And, no offense to your trustees, but these orders come from a Higher Authority. I've got my work authorization right here. (*Shows a slip to minister.*)

Minister: Well, since you're going to do it, can you at least tell me what the "Righteousness Cleaning" entails?

Malachi: Start with this Fullers' Soap. (*Holds up box with "Fullers' Soap" written on it.*) Strongest soap we got. Hope that cleans it. Not sure it will, though. Major defiling been goin' on here.

Minister: So, if the soap doesn't work, you're done, right?

Malachi: Wrong. Then we use fire.

Minister: Fire!

Malachi: Refiner's fire. Works great on gold and silver. Should work here, too.

Minister: Sounds dangerous. Not to mention painful.

Malachi: Can't promise you'll be the same, lady. Can tell you that The One who gives the orders will be pleased. Joyful, even.

Minister: I guess that's all we can do—live to make God joyful. I've noticed when we do that, we feel joyful too. Still, seems like a lot of work to go through.

Malachi: Lady, this is only the beginning!

Not Just for Prophets
Zephaniah: Cheerleader

Minister: Well, here we are in the third Sunday in Advent, and I think we can finally take a break from all those prophets. After all, the third Sunday in Advent is traditionally an upbeat, happy Sunday when we lighten up the tone from all that "Watch out, God is coming" stuff. And if there's one thing I can say about the prophets, it's that they certainly aren't very cheery. . . .

Zephaniah: (*Coming in from the side, out of direct view of the minister, dressed as a cheerleader.*) Hey everybody! Get ready to cheer for God!!

(*Zephaniah can improvise goofy cheerleading moves as he or she chants*)
We've been bad, but God is good—
God will act like we all should—
Judgment's not the final word—
There's good news, have you not heard?!

Renewed in love! Rejoicing above!
Save the lame! No more shame!
All our sadness . . . turned to gladness!
No fear! God's here! Leeeeeet's . . . CHEER!

Minister: Wait a minute, who the heck are you and WHAT do you think you're doing?

Zephaniah: I'm your prophet this week, silly! I'm Zephaniah! (*To the kids*) Can you say Zephaniah? Very good! But can you spell it! Gimme a Z! Gimme an E! Gimme a PH!

Minister: (*Interrupting*) Listen, we're trying to get ready for Christmas here. I don't really think we have time to build a cheerleading squad!

Zephaniah: Well, maybe you should rethink that! You see, I know people have a hard time remembering what's really important and keeping their priorities straight. They had those problems back in ancient Israel when I was a prophet there. But the whole point of all the naming and blaming we prophets do is to stop everyone from thinking about

38

themselves all the time, and to start thinking about God. And that's why we prophets aren't just about tears . . . we're about CHEERS TOO! Ready. . . . Let's go!

No fear! God's here! Yea . . . GOD!

Minister: I'm sorry, but I still don't really get it. I mean, I know it's fun to jump around with pom-poms and everything, but what does cheering have to do with getting ready for God to come into our lives?

Zephaniah: It's not so hard—and any kid will be able to tell you. Right, kids? When you are really, really looking forward to something great, the problems of your day-to-day life don't bother you so much. It's all about priorities, buddy, any prophet will tell you that. It's just that I like to shout a little more than those other guys.

(*Addressing the congregation*) Okay everybody, this cheer is easy and you can all do it! Hand in the air—now. Repeat after me . . .

No fear! God's here! Yea . . . GOD!

Not Just for Prophets
Micah: Hiker

(*Minister has been talking with young people for Story for All Ages. Minister and young people should all be sitting down at this time. Micah enters wearing hiking clothes—shorts, hiking boots, fleece jacket, bandana, and a hiking pack.*)

Whew. That last half mile was really a killer. This has been a long journey—feels at least three weeks since we started back at the trailhead.

(*Noticing the young people gathered for the Story for All Ages.*) Oh, hello there. Have you seen the rest of my group? Have they come by here yet? (*Kids answer "No."*)

Well, that's okay. I figured as much. You see, there was a bunch of us who started this hike, lots of folks from the house of Jacob, people from Jerusalem, not to mention Kings Jotham, Ahaz, and Hezekiah of Judah. A pretty good crowd. But, you know how it can go when you're on a long hike, especially on a mountain like this one that just seems to get harder and harder. They started fighting over who got to eat the M&Ms out of the trail mix and who had the best trail guide. Next thing you know, they're fighting over who knows God best and whipping out their swords and spears.

I said to them, "Guys, what are you doing packing all that extra weight around? It's slowing you down. It's keeping you from getting to God's temple. We started this climb to see God's promises revealed! Get rid of those weapons! You ought to change those swords into skateboards. And, while you're at it, change those spears into bicycles."

And you know something, I think they listened. This journey has changed them. Once they lighten their load, they'll be able to hike up the rest of this mountain in no time.

(*Looking at kids again*) But what about you guys? How come you haven't bagged this peak yet? Do you need to leave some stuff behind that is slowing you up? Or do you just need someone to go before you?

How about this? (*Takes out Bible and looks in it.*) We're already above tree line, and, you know, according to my guidebook, the summit is not far from here. While you figure out what you need to leave behind, I'll go around this next bend and see what's up there. I'll let you know what I see.

(*Hikes along and climbs up on a stool. Holds hand up to eyebrow.*) Oh, wow. The view is amazing from here! I can see everything from here, all of God's creation. And, all of creation is pointing in one place, to this stable that's got a big star shining over it. It's just a simple stable but everyone is moving toward it. Everyone—the hurt and the homeless, the bruised and the banished. Everyone who has ever been cast off or told they don't matter. They are like sheep all coming home to be fed. They can't wait to get to the stable. This view is incredible, more beautiful than I ever imagined it could be.

(*Hollering down to the kids*) Hey, you guys, you got to see this. More than that, you've got to experience this. Come on!

Interactive Sermons

The End of Nap Time

When I (HKD) was a child, I knew it was time for the sermon because the ushers dimmed the lights in the sanctuary. This practice made complete sense to me because the sermon was, after all, when my father took his nap. He'd stay awake for the minister's opening joke (which usually involved "little Johnny" in Sunday school) and then his head would start to bob—once, twice, and then he was out. The offertory woke him up again. That's when the lights came back up, and the organ brought everyone to their feet.

For most of those who attend worship at our churches (including those who do not actually lose consciousness), the sermon is a time in the service when they expect to sit back and let someone else do the work. They know they have to stand up for hymns, and they're prepared to shake someone's hand during the Passing of the Peace. But when the sermon comes around, they expect to be able to settle into the pew, let their thoughts drift, tune in and tune out, however the spirit moves them.

Well, no more. If we want worship to be different—less passive, less remote, more personal, more transformative—then we will have to preach differently. The most basic reason is this: the sermon, in many of our churches, is at the heart of our worship service. Even in congregations that have Communion every week, the sermon feels like the main event to many of our parishioners because it is the part that changes every week, the part that the minister seems to have spent the most time preparing.

In light of this, it absolutely must reflect the values that guide and shape the rest of the worship experience. If it doesn't, it will actually undermine all of our other efforts at change.

In addition to this basic reason, we could add a dozen others. Consider, for example, the work that has been done in recent decades about different styles of learning—only a minority of people in our congregations learns best by listening alone. Consider the model of the most effective teachers you know—chances are, they encourage their students to become active participants in the learning process. Consider your expectations of the response your sermon might provoke. If you are aiming higher than simply informing, amusing, or impressing your congregation with your insight and knowledge—if you want to provoke a response that might make a difference in their lives and in our world—then it's time to stop presenting a lecture about scripture and start involving your congregation in an interactive sermon.

Because the sermon is, in most of our congregations, the job of the minister alone, we don't recommend you start your process of worship transformation here. Start with things that involve more people (like the short dramas we've described in earlier chapters) and you'll build more allies for the change process. The congregation will have a sense of a group of people leading the change effort, and not make the worship leader the focus of all of their responses and reactions. But for the same reason, you will need to start preaching differently fairly early in the process of worship transformation. It is essential that you model your own willingness to change, your own openness to experimentation, and your own expectation that worship can be a practice that involves the whole congregation from start to finish.

What Do We Pay You to Do, Anyway?

For those of us who are professional clergy, the hardest part about preaching interactively is the sense that the sermon is the time each week when we earn our keep. Of all our work, it seems like the most legitimate. Who hasn't used the excuse "I'm working on my sermon" to avoid the phone, the office, housework, dental appointments, etc. It works! Sermon writing seems like something we should do without distractions, in a silent office surrounded by scholarly tomes. If we start asking our congregations what they think about a piece of scripture, if we invite them to weigh in on a theological point, what did we spend our week doing anyway? For that matter, what were all those years of theological education about?

To all of you who have had these thoughts, we have one simple piece of advice. Get over it. Your preaching will be a lot better if it stops being a time when you (consciously or subconsciously) show everyone how great you are. Start using it to model what it means to bring your whole life into conversation with God's word in scripture and beyond. And then invite your congregation to join you in that activity.

Are You with Me? Are You with Me?

An interactive sermon is also deeply challenging to your congregation. You're asking them to participate with you in the part of the service that is almost entirely reserved for the "experts." By asking them to do some of the interpretive work with you, you're suggesting to them that they are expert too. They have insight into life, intuitions about scriptures, and experiences of God that are key to understanding God's word to us this day. But you're also making it quite clear that you are not going to do all the work for them. This may not be entirely good news.

We've both gotten great backhanded compliments on our preaching. When Nancy started preaching at one congregation, a congregant said through clenched teeth on the way out of worship, "I can tell you're going to keep us on our toes." And someone told Heather that listening to her preach was like having someone snap her fingers in front of his face while saying, "Pay attention! Pay attention! Pay attention!" It's not so easy to pay attention through a whole sermon, and staying on your toes for any length of time isn't entirely comfortable.

So every step you make toward preaching in a more interactive manner has to be accompanied by lots and lots and lots of affirmation and praise. "Wow, you all have a lot of good insights!" "Thanks—those were hard questions to talk about, weren't they?" "Man do I appreciate you taking that risk!" "I really learned something from you all today!"

In addition, be sure to find another place for what the congregation loses when you begin to preach differently. If people complain that they miss your old style of preaching, press them to explain what they really valued about that time. They might want more teaching about theology or biblical interpretation—if so, invite them to join an adult education class. If one doesn't exist, invite them to form one with you. Or, they might miss some time for quiet meditation—time when they really can just let their thoughts wander. We all need quiet time, and if we name that as a positive value of our congregation, we can find the time and place for it, and still preach differently.

What follows are a variety of techniques for inviting your congregation to be part of your sermon. These techniques are listed in order of challenge to the preacher and to the congregation. But they are not necessarily steps that you need to move through sequentially. Depending on the scripture, the theme of the sermon, or our mood, we may use any one of these techniques on a given Sunday, or even use several.

Take a Vote

From the time we were in preschool and someone asked, "Who here likes ice cream?" we knew to raise our hands high to express our preferences. This comes so naturally for many of us that we will raise our hands if a waitress asks, "Who'd like a refill?" With that conditioning, it's no big stretch to get your congregation to do just this—raise their hands in answer to a question that you pose in your sermon. "Who here doesn't like snakes?" you ask as you begin to talk about Genesis 2, almost as an aside. "Who here has ever been rock climbing?" you ask, as if you're checking to see if at least someone will understand the metaphor for the spiritual life you're about to use.

You can begin this way—checking in with your listeners here and there during your sermon as if to see if they're following your point. If you not only pose the question, but actually ask for a show of hands in response, you're beginning to challenge your congregation's understanding of a sermon as your work, your words. You're expressing to them in a gentle way your expectation that they will be working and thinking right along with you. A sermon, you'll suggest, is something I need you to do with me.

If it seems like only some people are "voting," you can give them a little push—"Really? Only ten of you? Anyone else?" "Go ahead and raise your hand—I'm really curious!"

Take it one step further, and give the congregation two options and ask them to vote their preference. "Would you rather be with Jesus on the mountaintop or be with him in the valley?" we've asked on Transfiguration Sunday. "If you could only have one, would you rather have Christmas or Easter?" "Would you rather live in a rural area like Galilee or in a big city like Jerusalem?" Begin a sermon on the Beatitudes by asking, "Would you rather be rich or poor? Well-respected or reviled? Joyful or mourning?" Then ask everyone how Jesus would have voted.

You can have some fun as you survey your responses, commenting on husbands and wives who vote differently, or promising that the debate will continue at coffee hour. Or at the next meeting of the church council.

If you really want to have fun with voting, give your congregation a red, yellow, and green card in their program one morning and have them vote by holding up a card (red means disagree, green means agree, and yellow means not sure). We preached a sermon on church and culture this way, asking the congregation to vote on the statement, "The church needs to present the gospel in ways that resonate with contemporary culture" both at the beginning, during the middle, and at the end of the sermon. Of course, we presented various arguments both for and against the statement during the sermon, and people changed their votes as the sermon went on.

By the end, people were holding up red, green, or yellow cards even when they weren't asked to, and the voting continued during the final hymn (a mix of red and green), the organ postlude (green) and into coffee hour. Everyone was engaged that day!

Ask a "Warm-up" Question

It's only a small step to go from taking a vote to asking individuals to explain their vote. You can ask, "Who here has ever ridden a horse?" and take a vote. Then ask, "Do you remember what it felt like the very first time?" See if anyone nods, smiles, leans over to whisper to her neighbor. Then ask, "Does anyone have a story he'd like to share about the first time he was ever on a horse?"

Or you can ask for a vote and then notice someone who's voting differently than you expected. "Gladys, have you really been rock climbing? Good for you! Care to tell us about it?"

When done well, this is one of the best ways we've ever found for getting our congregations connected to the topic of our sermon. Just about any sermon suggests a "warm-up" question. Here are just a few of the many that we've used:

- What's your favorite part about the Christmas season?
- Have you ever discovered a talent you didn't think you had?

- What do you do when you're worried about something?
- Who was the best teacher you ever had?
- Have you ever looked for something only to discover it was right in front of your face?
- Have you ever had a dream come true?
- Have you ever had to leave something precious to you behind when you moved or traveled?
- Can you think of a time when you really felt at home somewhere other than your own home? What made you feel that way?
- Can you think of a time when you had "just enough"—neither too much, nor too little of something? Can anyone tell a story about that?

Our questions are often fun to think about, and provide occasions for people to share a funny story. In this regard, they take the place of those warm-up jokes about Little Johnny in Sunday school. They get people engaged, and often get people laughing.

But we never ask a question that is just an invitation to share funny experiences. Every question has a deeper side too, and that part is usually our lead-in to our sermon. Thus, every question becomes a gentle reminder to the congregation that their lives and their stories are keys to deeper insight about things that really matter.

For this reason, we never ask a question where there is clearly a "right" answer. Questions of that sort ask the congregation to play a bit part in the preacher's show. (Do you know the joke about the preacher who asks the children, "What's grey and has a fluffy tail and collects nuts in the fall?" A child raises his hand and says, "Well, it sure sounds like a squirrel, but I bet the right answer is Jesus!") The kinds of questions we seek to ask are ones that build a sense of community between the preacher and the congregation, and among the congregation.

The first time you realize that coffee hour is abuzz with people talking about their best teachers or their secret talents, you may feel a bit miffed that people paid more attention to your question than they did the rest of your finely crafted sermon. Don't go too far down that road! Instead, congratulate yourself for prompting some honest sharing among your congregation, and be absolutely sure to note your observation, with lots of approval, at the start of your next sermon. ("I loved hearing you talk about your teachers last week! You know, when you tell a story like that to someone else, either here in our sanctuary or even downstairs at coffee hour, you take a risk. Thanks so much for taking that risk!")

Invite an Action at the End of the Sermon

We come from churches that do not have altar calls. But we have to confess that sometimes we have altar-call envy. Our preaching is propelled by our conviction that God can change people, and so we are constantly on the lookout for creative ways to invite our congregation to respond positively to that invitation.

There are scores of ways to invite your congregation to do something at the end of a sermon to indicate their willingness to accept the challenge, or to make the commitment, or to engage in the question that was the focus of the sermon. Even churches that have occasional or regular altar calls might want to try one of these variations to approach that tradition in a fresh way. In every case, be clear that each one of these activities is optional. Extend an invitation and then let there be some open time in the service, perhaps accompanied by music, when people can choose to respond.

Here are some examples of things we've tried:

- On a Sunday before the beginning of Lent, preach a sermon about making a Lenten commitment that would help people take the "next step" on their spiritual journeys. After giving some examples of commitments of this sort, pass out footprints cut out of poster board along with black markers. Ask everyone who feels comfortable doing so to write his or her Lenten commitment out on the footprint and then to bring it to the altar to be blessed. Later, post these footprints all over the walls of the sanctuary, or in the hallways, or in the room where you hold coffee hour. Leave them up for all of Lent—they will be powerful reminders to take the commitments seriously.

- Place a number of boxes at the front of your sanctuary, only one of which is labeled "life" (the others might be blank, or they may have other labels which come from your sermon). Preach on Moses' final charge to the Israelites at the end of Exodus. ("Choose life that you and your descendants may live.") After interacting with the congregation about what it might mean for a community to chose life over death, roll out a shopping cart (if you "borrow" one from the food store, be sure to return it!) and invite a volunteer from the congregation to put the "life" box into the shopping cart. It's a simple gesture—but it makes the message of the sermon all the more clear.

- On a Sunday when you're preaching on the parable of the prodigal son, ask the congregation to take off their shoes when you describe the son's desperate state before he returns home. Then, tell about the father's embrace and his gift of shoes to his wayward son, and reflect on the honor such a gift symbolized in the ancient world. At the end of the sermon, invite the congregation to put their shoes back on with gratefulness for the love and honor God gives to each of us, no matter how far we've wandered.
- On a Sunday after Christmas, reflect on how the magi went home by a different way after seeing the baby Jesus. What would it mean for us to do the same in our spiritual lives? As a symbol of our willingness to be changed by our encounter with Jesus, ask everyone to leave the sanctuary using a different door from the one by which they entered. Suggest they might try walking or driving home by a different route as well. The following week, ask everyone how it went—some people may have gotten lost in their own neighborhoods!
- Explore ways in which your Communion service might flow directly out of your sermon. Then, asking the congregation to come forward to receive Communion becomes an invitation to grow in their intimacy with God and their capacity to live out their faith in the world.

Questions for Pairs

The questions we use as openers are ones that people can share without a great deal of thought, or without needing to tell particularly long stories. Not all questions are suited to this kind of sharing. Some questions are important to consider, but they require more time or more intimacy to answer. We don't shy away from those questions, but we make more room for them. And we don't start here—this kind of interaction works best when our congregations have really bought into the idea of working together as a community to reflect on God's word and respond.

Be sure that everyone has someone with whom to share! You might want to ask some lay leaders in advance to be "rovers," looking out for those who don't have a partner. Be sure to encourage everyone to pair not just with the people next to them in the pew, but also those who are in front of them or behind them.

Here's an example of questions we've used in this way:

- What's your favorite line in the Twenty-third Psalm? Why? You can use this question for just about any well-known scripture passage.
- Have you ever caught a glimpse of heaven?
- Describe a "holy moment" in your life.
- Describe a time when you felt like you were "outside the gate" (for a sermon on Acts 16).
- Share your image of what it might mean for God's "kingdom" to come.
- Share a favorite Christmas memory. Then share something that is hard about Christmas this year (for an Advent sermon, or for a sermon on the Sunday after Christmas).

Words of Warning

1. You may get answers you don't expect and answers that don't really work with the rest of your sermon. This has happened to us more than we like to admit, and it will certainly happen to you. Here's what we recommend:

- Whatever you do, don't debate with the person. Don't push him to look at it a different way, or suggest that she probably means something else.
- Don't dwell on the point. Just thank the person for sharing, and ask if there are any other stories, or if anyone else would like to share.
- If the answer really catches you by surprise, laugh! Tell the person, "Wow, that's an answer I didn't expect! We'll have to talk more about that later!" Then move on. Don't let the "wrong" answer attract so much attention that the rest of the congregation starts thinking in that direction too.
- Don't pretend the comment wasn't made. For example, you may have decided to begin your sermon by asking, "Recall a time when you did something for the first time. What did it feel like?" Someone may raise her hand and talk about the thrill she gets out of trying new recipes. This may inspire others to share positive first-time experiences. If this is what people have said, you cannot begin your sermon by saying, "It's always scary to do something for the first time," even if that's what you've planned on saying. Either ask if others have felt differently when faced with a new experience, or begin by saying, "Well, unlike a lot of you, I'm a person who sometimes finds beginnings scary. . . . "

2. You may have to interrupt people or cut people off. We all have people in our congregation who love to hear themselves talk. A phone call to check on a date for a meeting requires no less than forty-five minutes. When those folks raise their hands to share a story, everyone in the congregation inwardly groans.

You do not need to call on everyone. You can blatantly ignore the long-winded ones. (If you have a free afternoon, you might want to find them at coffee hour and ask to hear their story then, but we don't think that's strictly necessary.) You also have the right to cut people off. You might wait until they take a breath, or you might just interrupt them with a comment like, "We'll have to hear the rest of that story later, John. Does anyone else have a brief story to tell?"

This may sound rude, and in other contexts, it is. But this is not a town meeting or an open discussion. This is a sermon, and you are inviting the congregation to interact with you in your preaching. But you are in charge because you are the preacher. People are participating at your invitation.

If you let someone talk for too long, you are letting that person take control of the sermon time. The congregation has not willingly given them that power—they gave it to you, and it's not really yours to give away. Maintaining control during an interactive sermon is respectful of your congregation as a whole, even it if feels rude to an individual congregant in the moment.

In addition, if someone regularly uses your invitation to interact during the sermon as an opportunity to talk at great lengths or to go off on tangents, you will lose all support for this practice, and for other attempts at interaction as well. So have fun, but beware.

3. If you ask a question, you have to listen to the answers. That may sound obvious, but it can be really hard to do when you're also thinking about your sermon and evaluating each answer according to whether it fits in with your point or not. So do what you need to do to make it so you can really listen. Beginning with a clear sense of the main point of your sermon helps a lot. Don't try to construct (or deconstruct) your central thesis while you're standing there, getting input from your congregation. It also helps if you give the question period a time limit. And it helps if you can take a deep breath and trust the process. Your sermon will be better—even if the responses you get are not exactly the ones you hoped for. Trust that the Holy Spirit is at work in you and among your congregation, redeeming both your and their attempts to witness to God in your lives.

If you really do listen, and if you can remember key parts of some of the stories people tell, you can strengthen your sermon dramatically by referring back to the images and feelings evoked by the stories as you preach. It's even better if you can recall a story using the name of the person who told it.

It is possible to ask questions, and to incorporate answers, even if you preach with a manuscript. Just leave some blank spaces where you can insert a story if one arises.

When you demonstrate to your congregation your curiosity about their perspective on the important questions in life and your willingness to learn from them, even in the moment of preaching itself, you give them a powerful gift! In our experience, congregations will feel affirmed by the preacher's interest, and will respond by bringing more and more of their selves into worship.

4. Don't ask questions you're not willing to answer yourself. You don't necessarily have to answer every one of your own questions in detail, but you need to be willing to do so. Don't obviously evade the question. If others have taken real risks in their sharing, you can honor their vulnerability by meeting them there and being vulnerable yourself.

5. Don't try to trump everyone else's story. If you share your story after others have shared theirs, remember not to do so in a way that suggests your experience is the real or true one. Be careful about this especially if you're a really good storyteller. You may want to put some space between the stories of the congregation and your story—tell yours at the end. And you may want to simply keep your story in reserve if it is somehow more intense or "spiritual" than the stories others have shared. If someone in your congregation tells a really powerful story, take a moment to be quiet and let the story sink in. It may be that the story just preached the gospel in a way that you never could have that morning. Be thankful, and honor the story by not following it up with a joke.

6. If it doesn't work, move on. Sometimes people may not have much to say about your question. It might be that no one has ever played in a marching band, or waited for bread to rise, or walked on a tight rope. So be it. Laugh with your congregation a bit about that ("Okay, we'll have to bring the circus trainers in for our next deacon's retreat!") and move on.

7. Once people have your permission to talk to you during your sermon, they may do so without your prompting. This hasn't become a huge problem for us, but it does happen occasionally. Once the taboo against speaking during the sermon time is broken, people do occasionally call out a comment here and there even when we haven't asked them a question. Don't allow for a sermon takeover, but don't panic either. The person might be making a good point!

INTERACTIVE CONFESSIONS AND ASSURANCES OF PARDON

The Predicament of the Pronouncement

As a Congregationalist, I (HKD) am part of a tradition that's sometimes called "Low Church Protestant." That is to say, ministers in my tradition are more like teachers and organizers than they are like priests. No
special robes or rules for me—I'm just one of the folks. But when I began
serving my last congregation, a tradition there caught me by surprise and
made me examine even my "low church" assumptions about what the
minister's job should be. In that church, after the congregation read
together a Prayer of Confession, a lay leader gave the Assurance of
Pardon.

Is that the right way to do it, I wondered? The Assurance of Pardon,
the statement that the congregation's sins are forgiven, seemed to me like
one of the few times in worship when we would want things to look as
"official" as possible. It wasn't, after all, a time for someone to share his or
her opinion that people in the congregation were basically okay (an
opinion that I'm not even sure my lay leaders held). The Assurance of
Pardon was in fact the place where people were reminded that it was
God's Official Policy that all who sincerely confess are forgiven. In
Christ, we are all new creations! Thanks be to God!

But after fretting about how I might discuss this with the deacons for a
number of months, one Sunday I actually listened to what the lay leader

that morning was saying. In a quiet but clear voice, a young woman looked up from her page and said, "Friends, believe the good news of the gospel: in Jesus Christ, we are forgiven." And it struck me—she wasn't pronouncing something with the authority that came from a role or a title. The only way she could say those words with the simple clarity and conviction she had was if she had experienced forgiveness herself. Her words, as a result, were deeply inviting.

As in the rest of worship, in our time of confession and assurance, our actions often speak louder than our words. We must show in the way this part of the service is conducted that reconciliation is an experience and not just an idea. It has a story. It connects to our lives. It is active and interactive. It is communal.

Years later, I was again surprised by the impact of community-led confession and pardon during the morning worship in the Abbey on the island of Iona, Scotland. There, the cooks and chambermaids and administrative staff and groundskeepers of the Iona Community all take turns leading the morning liturgy. The worship leader first says the simple confession, and the entire congregation responds, "May God forgive you, Christ renew you, and the Spirit enable you to grow in love." Then, the congregation says the same confession, and the leader responds back with the same words. The circle of confession and forgiveness made it clear—we do not do this work alone, and we cannot do this work for another. The work of reconciliation with God and with each other is something we must do together.

What would it mean to invite people to experience forgiveness instead of just pronouncing them forgiven? Below are some things we've tried, ranging from small and simple to full-scale productions.

The Power of Silence

Someone once told me that the most inclusive form of prayer is silence. It is especially fitting to carve out some silent space before or after a spoken prayer of confession. Because time tends to fly when you're standing up front, we often time our silent periods, or ask our lay leaders to do so. One minute is a minimum, and two minutes (which can feel excruciatingly long at first) allows us to really feel the quiet settle into the sanctuary.

If your congregation has trouble with silence, or if you'd like to vary the experience, offer a suggestion as to how to use the time. Remind everyone to breathe deeply through their noses. Suggest that they "listen" to the silent room. Suggest they imagine themselves resting by the "still waters" of Psalm 23, or leaning gently on Jesus who is sitting in the pew next to them.

Tell the Story

The best way to relate an idea to an experience is to tell a story. Resist the temptation to make a whole sermon out of it—the simpler, the better. For example, retell a well-known Bible story (the prodigal son, Jesus and the woman caught in adultery, Joseph's reconciliation with his brothers) and draw out of it an invitation to see our own lives through the lens of the story. Or, offer a simple story from your own life. The point is not to make a production out of confessing your own sinfulness. The point is to provide an image or an illustration that others in your congregation can connect to their own lives and relate to their own experience.

One of my favorite confessions and assurances of pardon was simply a two-part story shared by a lay leader in my congregation. In the first part, told as an introduction to the congregational prayer of confession, the speaker told a story of repeatedly forgetting the name of the owner of a local flower shop with whom she had a number of conversations that week. Since a number of people in the congregation knew the woman whose name she had forgotten, her story brought a few laughs, in part because it was something we could have so easily done. Our shared confession then highlighted our inattentiveness to each other, and to God.

Then, after the refrain of a song and a few moments of silence, the speaker told of her awkward attempt to apologize to the person whose name she could not remember—and her inability to remember her name even in the midst of her apology. Again we laughed, but there were tears in our eyes as we did so. The leader told the story with such humility that it became an invitation for each of us to connect with tenderness to our own fumbling attempts to do right by each other, and by God.

Sing It—From Start to Finish

Some of the old hymns say it best. "Just as I am, without one plea, . . . O Lamb of God, I come." "Amazing Grace, how sweet the sound!" A great way to deepen the experience of confession and pardon, to slow it down and make the experience more prayerful, is to insert sung refrains after each section. Or, simply replace any spoken confession with a verse from a hymn, and allow the congregation to experience the hymn as their prayer. This is especially effective if you can find a hymn that many people in your congregation know by heart (for example, "Amazing Grace").

Make It Physical

Eyes, Mouth, Ears: As you read a prayer of confession together, invite the congregation to cover their eyes as you speak about our blindness to the wonder of the world around us, their mouths as you speak about our rash judgments and careless words, and their ears as you speak about our deafness to the cries of those in need.

Closed Fist, Open Hand: Invite the congregation to read a corporate prayer of confession with their fists clenched hard. In the silence that follows, invite them to slowly unclench their fists and open up their hands. Then, after the assurance of pardon, invite them to shake hands with one another.

Kneeling, Standing: Try praying in a new posture. If your congregation doesn't regularly kneel during prayer, suggest that some might try it one Sunday (in the aisles if the construction of your pews makes it impossible). Or try praying standing, with arms reaching out in a gesture of supplication. These postures are all the more powerful if they are held for a few moments of silence.

Make It Interactive

Write it down: You might make this option available one Sunday, or every Sunday. Include slips of paper in the pew or in the program, and invite people to write particular confessions down, assuring them of their confidentiality. You might collect these slips in baskets, or invite people to come forward and lay them on the altar, or at the base of a cross. Pray over the papers—and be sure to touch them as you do.

Or get creative. For example, on a Sunday focused on Jesus' call to Peter and James, say a few words about what we have to leave behind to follow Jesus. Inside each order of worship that week include a small boat simply folded out of origami paper. For your prayer of confession, ask everyone to write on the paper boats what he or she needs to leave behind. Then, sing the hymn "Lord, You Have Come to the Lakeshore" ("now my boat's left on the shoreline behind me; by your side I will seek other seas.") As the music continues, invite people to come forward and leave their boat on the altar. There will be very few dry eyes in the congregation!

Say it out loud: While it is hard for a group much larger than ten to offer individual prayers of confession out loud, it is possible to do so with some specific instruction. For example, suggest that people say out loud a single word that might speak to something they would like to confess (Jealous. Lonely. Ignore. Want.). Follow that prayer with an assurance of pardon, and an invitation to speak words of assurance to each other (Found. Loved. Known.).

For even more inspiration, look ahead to our interactive Ash Wednesday service. Any one of the activities suggested could be used in worship as a new way to experience confession and forgiveness.

Go Hog Wild

Sometimes, it's good to suspend the rules. Who says the Confession and Assurance of Pardon should only take three or four minutes? It often feels to us like the most important work we need to do as Christians each week, and we long to linger there, really noticing what we're doing and why. So why not make it the most engaging, most memorable part of the worship service? With that idea in mind, we developed **Changed and Challenged by Jesus,** a series that (believe it or not) uses homemade, parade-sized puppets to lead the congregation to a whole new experience of repentance and forgiveness. It's seven weeks long, and designed to be used during Lent. But with some adaptation, you could use it any time of the year.

Just to clarify: this series goes way beyond the usual confession and assurance of pardon. As we wrote, it expanded to include the Story for All Ages time and can serve as a good portion of the Gospel reading as well. Each segment of the series is at least ten minutes long.

Sound a little wild? Well, it is. But in our experience, the creativity of this series breaks something open in the hearts of our congregation. Each time we've used it, it has led to wonderful conversations, deep reflections, and a new appreciation of some well-known Bible stories. Give it a try— or let it be a spur to your own imagination. What can you imagine happening in worship if you let confession and forgiveness take up all the time and space they deserve?

Changed and Challenged by Jesus: A Lenten Series of Interactive Bible Stories, Confessions, and Assurances of Pardon

Introduction

This series was designed to make use of parade-sized puppets that are worn on backpacks by adults and teens hidden under the puppet's cloth body. Intergenerational teams from your congregation can make puppets of this sort over the course of two hour-and-a-half workshops, and they will have a great time doing it. While a construction project of this scale may seem daunting, we can assure you that it is worth it!

People in our congregations, regardless of their age, have been touched and excited by the experience of building and then worshiping with big puppets. Children remember the Bible stories these puppets tell, and want to tell the stories to others. Adults want to hug and touch the puppets and even have their pictures taken with them. Older adults, or those who sit in the back of the church, who sometimes have a hard time seeing what is going on up front, feel completely included during this Lenten series. Everyone tells their friends about the wonderful thing that is happening at their church this year. Your local newspaper may want to run a story!

That said, it is by all means possible to use this series in other ways. You can use simple hand puppets. You can use people in costumes to pantomime the story. Consider making something large—a large cardboard mask on a wooden stick, for example. Whatever you do, consider ways in which you might involve teams from your congregation in designing and constructing the mask, puppet, or costume that will be used.

Materials (if you are planning to build parade-sized puppets)

- Begin by asking around your community to see if there is a local puppeteer with whom you might work. Be clear about what you're looking for, and you may eventually find someone who could lead

the workshops at your church, or at least train you and a small team.
- Step-by-step directions for puppet making are also readily available on the web. Either search under "giant puppet making directions" or check out:
    www.gis.net/~puppetco (extremely helpful)
    www.sagecraft.com/puppetry
    www.spiralq.org/resourcesHome.html
- You can also get information (including a very helpful video) by contacting Bread and Puppet at:
    Bread and Puppet Press
    753 Heights Road
    Glover, Vermont 05839

Supplies that most directions call for include:
- 4 boxes of cornstarch.
- Old newspaper.
- Brown paper grocery bags (lots).
- Two refrigerator boxes. Your local appliance store will be happy to save them for you if you just ask.
- Staple pliers. Florists use them and they will know where to find them in your area.
- Scrap lumber.
- Old white sheets.
- Poster paints.
- A ¼ yard of white lace for creating the "see-through" spot on the puppets' bodies.
- Fun, sparkly fabric (scraps are great). Sparkly markers and glue. You will use this on Easter morning to decorate your puppets in honor of the resurrection.

Preparation

- Schedule two puppet-making days on the calendar. Preferably, the first one should be a month before the start of Lent and the second two weeks later. Advertise the puppet-making time in your newsletter and at worship. Puppet making is truly a multigenerational activity. People ages 2 to 92 can all participate and enjoy themselves. This is one activity where children and adults are on equal footing. It is especially great for youth groups along with other members of your church. Recruit widely!

- Find a place to make puppets where you have five individual tables to work on and where you can easily clean up the floor. Puppet making is not overly messy, but it's not a project for the Ladies' Parlor!
- Get directions for making the puppets. If you can get a puppeteer to come in and lead your puppet making, so much the better. If not, make sure that you and another member of the church understand how to do it.
- Gather up all your materials.
- Copy the scripture texts for the five Bible Friends (puppet friends) you will be making. If you can, laminate them so that they can be used for reference even when things start to get gooey at the workshop.
- At the puppet-making workshops, ask those present not to talk about or show the puppets to the rest of the congregation. Explain that you want people to be surprised when the first Bible Friend arrives.
- Ask members of your church to act out the different Lenten stories for each Sunday. Once the puppets are finished, be sure to schedule time to rehearse. Practice is key with large puppets! Note that the puppets are very tall—you may need to practice getting in and out of your sanctuary.

Things to Consider

- Preach on the theme of "Changed and Challenged by Jesus" for Lent. Most of the featured Bible passages are Gospel readings in the Revised Common Lectionary, Year A. Many of the ideas introduced in the series can be developed more fully in a sermon.
- Large puppets may be frightening at first to some younger children. Model your own comfort by physically interacting with the puppet. Consider having the puppet of the week join everyone at coffee hour after church. That way, children can find out that there is a real person inside.
- Have a blank book in the sanctuary ready as people come in where they can write their weekly experiences of being changed and challenged by Jesus. Or, invite people to write down such experiences as a small group exercise. Consider including these stories in your liturgy—as an introduction to worship, as an introduction to prayer, or as part of your sermon.
- Set aside special time in worship and ask people to give a short testimony of how Jesus has changed and challenged them in the past week.

How to Use the Scripts

- While the giant puppets don't speak, they do act. The parade-sized puppets can express themselves mostly through the use of their hands, and we have written stage directions into the scripts for the series with this in mind. When a word or phrase is in ALL CAPITALS, it indicates a gesture or a movement of the puppet. Sometimes we've suggested a particular movement, and sometimes we've simply capitalized a word that we think suggests a movement. There is plenty of room for improvisation. Just be sure to practice so that the puppet's movements are as BIG as the puppet is.
- In addition to the puppet, each script also calls for a narrator. The minister or other worship leaders might play this role, but they do not need to. The entire series can be cast with teens, for example. Note that the parade puppets are too large to be worn by children.
- On some Sundays, there is also a part for someone playing Jesus. We recommend simply inviting another lay leader or teen to read this part—no costume, and very little acting involved. Consider inviting a woman or a girl to read this part some weeks. While having a separate voice for Jesus makes the stories more easily understandable, the focus of the series is on the puppet—that is, the person who meets Jesus—and on the change that happens to him or her over the course of the story.
- Each Sunday, the interaction with the puppet leads to the congregational confession. These confessions should be printed in your Sunday bulletin and read in unison. We have included prayers that are especially appropriate to intergenerational worship. You may substitute prayers more familiar to your congregation.

Insert this series in your order of worship so that it precedes, and flows into, the Prayer of Confession and Assurance of Pardon. You will probably not want to include a separate Story for All Ages on the weeks you use this series.

On Easter, the Nicodemus puppet is the only one needed for the story that leads to the Confession and Assurance of Pardon. In addition to Nicodemus, we suggest that all six puppets come back into the sanctuary during the last hymn for an "Easter Parade" your congregation will not soon forget!

The Easter Parade is especially effective if each puppet is somehow transformed for Easter. This might mean something as simple as a sparkly piece of fabric draped around the shoulders of each puppet, or you could completely reclothe and redecorate each puppet (a great activity for the youth group).

Changed and Challenged by Jesus
Week 1: Nicodemus

Narrator: Good morning, everyone! I'd like to introduce you to a friend of mine. His name is Nicodemus. (*PUPPET BOWS.*) The Gospel of John has a great story to tell about the first time Nicodemus met Jesus. He really got challenged! (*PUPPET NODS.*)

Here's the story. Nicodemus was a man who spent most of his time studying God's laws and God's prophets. He liked to CONSIDER things. He liked to DEBATE things. He looked at problems from the ONE HAND and then from THE OTHER HAND. And you know what he liked best of all? He liked to figure things out!

Now, when Nicodemus heard about Jesus, and how he was teaching people about God, he went and KNOCKED on Jesus' door. He wanted to see if Jesus was as great as everyone was saying. Maybe he thought Jesus would DEBATE with him. Maybe he'd join Nicodemus looking at things from the ONE HAND and then from the OTHER HAND. And maybe, just maybe, he'd help Nicodemus figure things out!

Nicodemus started the conversation by COMPLIMENTING JESUS, saying that he was a teacher who came from God. Jesus responded,

Jesus: No one can see the kingdom of God without being born from above.

Narrator: And this confused Nicodemus entirely! (*PUPPET SCRATCHES HIS HEAD.*) How can anyone get born a second time? How can you go back to being a baby when you've already grown up? Nicodemus asked Jesus to explain himself, but the more he talked, the more confused Nicodemus got. (*PUPPET SPINS AROUND.*) Pretty soon HIS HEAD HURT! He asked him, HOW CAN THESE THINGS BE? Jesus responded simply,

Jesus: Are you a teacher of Israel, and yet you do not understand these things?

Narrator: And that's when Jesus started speaking, speaking to Nicodemus and speaking to you and me and everyone else who has ever wanted to figure things out. He told Nicodemus that he had to start looking at the world a different way. (*PUPPET "LOOKS" WITH HIS HAND TO HIS EYEBROWS.*) To begin with, he had to realize that there are some things that he wasn't going to figure out by thinking and talking. There are some things in the world that are mysterious.

And then Jesus told Nicodemus that there was one thing he could know for sure—love. Jesus told him that God had sent his Son to earth because God loves the world. And he told him that God's love gives us new life.

When Jesus said all of this, Nicodemus began to realize something. (*PUPPET JUMPS UP AND DOWN.*) His questions about God, his debates and discussions, were often a way for him to keep God at ARM'S LENGTH. Jesus was inviting Nicodemus to do more than to talk about God. Jesus showed him how to have a relationship with God. He showed him that God had EMBRACED HIM with love.

Have you ever wanted to keep God at a distance? Have you ever wanted to keep God in the Bible, or here in church, while you live your life as you feel like it? We're not so different from Nicodemus. Let's pray together now a prayer of confession, and ask God to forgive us. When we pray like this, we open ourselves up to God's love:

Prayer of Confession:
Loving God, we confess to you that we have not always been willing
    to welcome you into our lives.
Sometimes we would rather argue with you than do what you ask us to do.
Sometimes it seems safer to think about you than to love you.
Forgive us, God, and help us to live in a different way.
Help us to talk to you, but to listen too.
Help us to open our arms to you.
We know that you have invited us to live our lives for you.
Help us to accept the invitation.

Narrator: Nicodemus went back to his work after his discussion with Jesus that night, but he never forgot Jesus. In fact, the Gospel of John tells us that he defended Jesus when other people tried to bring charges against him in the Jewish courts of law. And Nicodemus was one of the people who stood by Jesus, even when his own followers had run away. Perhaps he had figured something out after all.

Jesus showed Nicodemus, in his life and in his death, how great God's love is. Love is stronger than sin, love is stronger than anything we could do to separate or distance ourselves from God. This is GOOD NEWS for all of us. We can trust that God forgives us, and welcomes us with OPEN ARMS.

Changed and Challenged by Jesus
Week 2: The Woman at the Well

Narrator: Good morning, everyone! I've got another friend to intro-duce to you today, the Woman at the Well. (*PUPPET CURTSIES.*)

Who here knows what a well is? (*PUPPET SHRUGS.*) (*Addressing puppet*) Who should we choose to answer the question? (*PUPPET POINTS TO A YOUNG PERSON.*) So, what is a well? You're right!

My friend here went to a well every day to get her water. She didn't have a sink like you and I do. Everyone in her community had to go to the well to get water. Water for DRINKING. Water for WASHING. Water for COOKING.

Now, there are a couple of important things I have to tell you about my friend. First of all, this woman here is a Samaritan. (*PUPPET NODS.*) Has anyone here ever heard of a Samaritan before? Some of you may have heard of the "Good Samaritan" from a story that Jesus told. From that name, "Good Samaritan," you might think that Samaritans are well-loved people. (*PUPPET NODS.*) Actually the opposite is true. (*PUPPET SHRUGS AND SHAKES HER HEAD.*) Back in Bible times, a lot of people thought that Samaritans were bad or dirty people. A lot of people didn't want to talk with them or even be near them.

The second thing I have to tell you is that the Woman at the Well didn't have many friends even within her own group, the Samaritans. Her neighbors didn't like her. She used to be embarrassed to SHOW HER FACE in public.

But on one particular day, something amazing happened at the well. As the woman CAME TO GET HER WATER, she could SEE there was a stranger at the well. As she came closer to the man, she could tell from the clothes he wore that he wasn't one of her kind, he wasn't a Samaritan. She wondered, "What is this strange man doing in my town?" (*PUPPET LOOKS AT JESUS AND SCRATCHES HER HEAD.*) The man said to her,

Jesus: Give me drink.

Narrator: Now, back then, people from Jesus' group wouldn't eat or drink with Samaritans, so the woman was surprised. (*PUPPET TURNS AWAY FROM JESUS.*) My friend said, "I am a Samaritan and you're not, so how can you ask me for a drink?" Jesus said,

Jesus: Please, I would love a drink. As soon as I have quenched my thirst, I'll tell you about the living waters of God.

Narrator: The woman was interested. She LEANED DOWN and FILLED her pitcher with water. Then she HANDED it to Jesus. Jesus drank deeply from the well. Then, as he rested from his journey, he told the woman that he could give her living water to drink. Although she was a bit confused by his words, she listened intently. (*PUPPET PUTS HER HAND TO HER EAR.*) She wanted this living water. (*PUPPET NODS.*) Indeed, she could already feel a great calm coming over her as she spoke to Jesus.

The more they talked, the more refreshed she felt. The woman at the well forgot all her worries about being a Samaritan and about being talked about in her town. She felt only LOVE IN HER HEART. She felt good about herself for the first time in a long time.

Before meeting Jesus, the Woman at the Well assumed God didn't want anything to do with her. (*PUPPET MAKES HAND GESTURE OF "NO WAY!"*) Because she met Jesus, now she knows the truth. We can tell God anything, and God will still love us. Like a beautiful, fresh, and clean stream, God's love is always flowing to us. Trusting in God's love, will you join with me in the confession written in your Order of Worship?

Prayer of Confession:
Gentle and Holy God, we confess to you that we have not loved ourselves as you have loved us. We have chosen to see ourselves through the mirror of disappointment, of failure, of unworthiness. We have forgotten we were created in your image, and, instead, have come to believe that we are unimportant and incapable of change.

Forgive us, O God. Open our eyes again to the truth of your Son, Jesus Christ. He came to redeem the world, even to redeem us! Help us again to see ourselves and all our brothers and sisters of the world through your loving eyes. Amen.

Narrator: My friend has never forgotten that amazing day. In fact, the Woman at the Well told her story to anyone who would listen. (*PUPPET RUNS FROM PERSON TO PERSON IN THE CONGREGATION, POINTING TO JESUS AND HUGGING HERSELF.*) Because of her, everyone learned that Jesus came for the whole world, not just a small group of people. Jesus told her that his love is like a river that will flow forever. That water comes from God's great well of forgiveness. It never empties; it is always waiting for us. Because of Jesus' love, we are awash in new life. Amen.

Changed and Challenged by Jesus
Week 3: The Man Who Was Lame

Narrator: Ladies and Gentlemen, we have a very special guest with us this morning. I'd like to introduce you to the Man Who Was Lame! (*PUPPET BOWS.*)

I can imagine what you're thinking—that was a pretty SMOOTH ENTRANCE for someone who's lame. Lame, after all, is a word they use in the Bible to describe just about any kind of problem with your legs. And that's what this man was like for almost all his life—until he met Jesus.

My friend here had an accident or injury when he was a kid that made it so his legs didn't work so well. And so, when he tried to walk, he walked LIKE THIS. As you can see, he didn't get very far very fast. Back in those days, there weren't wheelchairs to help him out. So this man had a hard time getting around, keeping up with other people. Can you imagine how that made him feel? That's right, he was really, really SAD.

The Man Who Was Lame was always LOOKING OUT for a way to get healed. He tried going to different doctors. He tried doing different EXERCISES (*have some fun here*). But nothing worked.

Then, one day, he heard about a special place in Jerusalem where people were getting cured of their illnesses. It was a pool, a little pond, right in the middle of that big city, and whenever the pool started to bubble, the person who got into the water first would be healed of whatever problem he or she had.

Well, when the Man Who Was Lame heard about this special pool he went there immediately. Of course, it took him a LONG TIME to get there. By the time he got there, the edges of the pool were already packed with other people who wanted to get cured of their illnesses. So the Man Who Was Lame had to stand way back from the pool, and from there it was pretty hard to see if the water was moving or not, and pretty hard to see if anyone was getting cured.

But the Man Who Was Lame didn't have any better ideas, so he waited. And waited. And pretty soon his poor legs were so tired that he had to SIT DOWN. And then it was even harder to try to get into the pool at the right moment. When he noticed people moving, he'd STRUGGLE TO HIS FEET and by then the bubbles had stopped and the moment to get healed was all over.

"If only someone would help me!" the Man Who Was Lame thought to himself. "If only someone would give me a PIGGYBACK RIDE down to the pool when the moment comes, then I could get healed." (What do you think, kids? Would anyone here like to volunteer to give this man a piggyback ride??)

The Man Who Was Lame realized that this would never happen. No one would ever help him. Because, after all, the people gathered at the side of the pool were sick too. If those people were to help the Man Who Was Lame, they would miss their own chance at healing. Only the first person in the pool was supposedly healed, and as long as everyone there wanted to be that first person, no one was going to help anyone else. *They all thought it was more important to heal themselves than it was to heal other people.*

So, he was stuck. And the Man Who Was Lame got stuck for a very long time at the side of that pool. He might have been there for years. The longer he stayed there, the madder he got at everyone else in the world. He blamed them for his problems, and he COMPLAINED TO EVERYONE WHO WOULD LISTEN.

Have you ever been there? Have you ever gotten stuck inside? Have you ever found yourself staying mad at someone? Holding onto a grudge? Blaming everyone around you for the problems of your life? It's real easy to do. But we know it's not where God wants us to be. Let's begin our healing together by confessing our sins to God:

Prayer of Confession:
Loving God, we come to you as wounded people. We say that we are looking for healing, but somewhere along the way, we have forgotten how to move. We are stuck—in our anger, our resentment, our jealousy, our fear. Sometimes we even forget that we want to be healed.

Forgive us, God, and give us a new spirit. Help us to remember that you want us to move and grow. Help us to hear your invitation to healing, and clear a path between us and the source of that healing, your Son, Jesus Christ.

Narrator: There's good news in this story, for the Man Who Was Lame, and for us. He didn't stay stuck at the side of that pool, because Jesus came to him. When Jesus saw him lying there, he knew his story—the years of struggle, the pain in his legs and in his heart, and he asked him one simple question.

Jesus: Do you want to be made well?

Narrator: At first the Man Who Was Lame was CONFUSED. He thought Jesus was asking him why he hadn't gotten into the pool already. He explained the difficulty he had moving, he explained the pushing and shoving of the other people, and he explained how it was impossible to get anyone to help him. (*PUPPET MAKES HIS COMPLAINING GESTURE.*) But Jesus must have heard something else in his voice as well— a yearning for wholeness, a desire to accept the invitation to a healed body and spirit. And so Jesus said to him simply,

Jesus: Stand up, take your mat, and walk.

Narrator: And that was that. The man was healed. He stood up and walked, SLOWLY AT FIRST, testing his legs, but soon he was SKIPPING and DANCING and SPINNING AROUND WITH JOY. It was only later that the Man Who Was Lame found out who had healed him. And it was much, much later, when the Man Who Was Lame heard about how Jesus had been crucified that he began to understand how different Jesus was from all the other people who had been at the pool with him. For Jesus, it really was more important to heal other people than to be healed. He loved the people of the world so much that he preferred to die rather than deny that love. He put his life on the line for others, plain and simple. And that kind of love has the power to heal, even here, even now. Thanks be to God!

Changed and Challenged by Jesus
Week 4: The Man Born Blind

Narrator: Hi, everybody, I'd like to introduce you to another friend of mine. Do you notice anything special about him? (*PUPPET TWIRLS AROUND AND VAMPS WHILE YOUNG PEOPLE GUESS WHAT IS SPECIAL ABOUT HIM.*)

Well, you made a lot of good guesses, but the thing that is most special about him is that he can see. Now, you might think that is no big deal. Who here can see? Well, that's something that my friend here couldn't do for most of his life. He was blind. (*PUPPET COVERS HIS EYES.*) So, the fact that my friend can see now is really amazing.

You might ask, how did a person who was blind suddenly start to be able to see? That is what I want to tell you about today.

One day, my friend was doing his errands in the market square of his town. Because he couldn't see, the man was FEELING HIS WAY ALONG. Suddenly, he TOUCHED the face of a stranger. The Man Born Blind didn't recognize the face. "Who is this man?" he wondered. (*PUPPET SHRUGS.*) Does anyone know who it was? That's right, Jesus!

After talking with his friends about the Man Born Blind, Jesus did something very surprising. He spat on the ground and made mud with his saliva and put it on the Man Born Blind's eyes. Gross, right? Except that it wasn't. It was soothing and cooling on the man's face. (*PUPPET RUBS HIS EYES.*)

Jesus then sent the man to go wash in a nearby pool (*PUPPET BENDS DOWN AND ACTS OUT WASHING HIS BODY*), and when he came out of the water, he could see! (*PUPPET JUMPS UP AND DOWN, CELEBRATING.*) People couldn't believe it! They kept asking, "Is that really you?" "Aren't you the one who was born blind?" "How come you can see?"

The man couldn't explain it. He said simply that the man named Jesus had healed him. He told everyone that. He expected them to be as joyous as he was. (*PUPPET TRIES TO GET PEOPLE IN THE CONGREGATION TO DANCE WITH HIM.*) What could be more wonderful than to be healed? But people started to argue about whether Jesus should have done what he did. The crowds of people questioned Jesus angrily. (*PUPPET SHAKES HIS HEAD AND WAVES HIS HANDS.*) I guess they were scared by the change that had taken place in my friend's life.

Things got so messy and mean that they eventually made the man leave town. And when that happened, the man hated all his old friends and neighbors. (*PUPPET SHAKES HANDS ANGRILY.*) He stormed out of there, cursing his neighbors under his breath as he went. (*PUPPET STOMPS DOWN THE AISLE.*) He let them all know that he wanted nothing more to do with them.

It turns out both the Man Born Blind and the people in his town had something in common. The townspeople didn't really believe he could change; and when the Man Born Blind stormed out of town, he showed that he didn't really believe the townspeople could change either. He gave up on them rather than staying with them.

It's hard to stay in relationships that require us to change! That's one of the things this story is all about. And it's one of the hard things about being a Christian, too. Sometimes we'd rather things stay broken and stay the same. Sometimes we'd rather run away than help someone see things in a new way. Won't you join with me in the Prayer of Confession printed in your Order of Worship?

Prayer of Confession:

We confess to you, O God, that we are in need of healing. We recognize that, as a church and as a society, we often lose sight of your message of love and mercy. Sometimes we run away from you rather than open ourselves up to the healing that you make possible to us every day. We would rather live as a broken people than to do the work of healing our communal wounds.

Challenge us to see how much we need your forgiving love. Aid us in making this community a holy dwelling of love, justice, and Christian community. We pray in the name of Jesus the Christ who, by his very love for us, allows us to see the world anew.

Narrator: The man left town, but that is not the end of the story. Jesus heard that the townspeople had driven the Man Born Blind out, and he came and found him. (*JESUS WALKS UP THE AISLE AND GETS THE PUPPET AND BRINGS HIM BACK TO THE FRONT.*) Because of what Jesus did, the man could see not only how people turn away from God, but also how God comes back to us. God doesn't leave us alone in our separation. (*PUPPET AND JESUS HOLD HANDS.*)

Jesus recognizes all our faults and problems, but he still loves us and wants us to be whole again. In him, we are forgiven and made whole. Amen.

Changed and Challenged by Jesus
Week 5: Lazarus

Narrator: Ladies and Gentlemen, I know you have enjoyed meeting all the special guests we have had from the Bible over the past month. Today, we're going to meet our very last guest, and he is an extremely special person. He's famous for one thing in particular: he died, and was buried, but three days later he came back to life. Can anyone guess the name of the person I'm talking about? (*Everyone guesses Jesus.*) No! Not Jesus! I'm talking about Lazarus. Here he comes now! (*PUPPET STRIDES ENTHUSIASTICALLY UP THE AISLE.*)

Looking at him, it's hard to believe he was once dead, isn't it? Well, here's what happened. Lazarus lived in a town not far from Jerusalem along with his sisters, Mary and Martha. The three of them led very active lives—RAKING and HOEING and HERDING SHEEP and CARRYING WATER and CHOPPING WOOD, and doing all of the things that people had to do back in those days just to live.

Well, somewhere along the line, Lazarus got sick. He got weaker and weaker. (*PUPPET SLOWS DOWN, THEN SINKS TO HIS KNEES.*) And soon everyone around him could see that he wasn't feeling well. By the time his sisters convinced him to rest, it was too late. Lazarus was dying.

Martha and Mary, Lazarus's sisters, knew just what to do. They sent a message to a good friend of theirs, someone who they knew had a very special relationship with God, someone who they knew had the power to heal people. Can anyone guess who that was? That's right! Jesus! They called out, "Jesus, we need you!"

But here's the strange thing: Jesus took his time in getting over to Lazarus's house. (*JESUS STARTS FROM THE BACK OF THE SANCTUARY AND SLOWLY COMES UP. HE STOPS TO SIT DOWN IN A FEW PEWS BEFORE GETTING TO THE FRONT WHERE THE PUPPETS ARE.*) His disciples wondered why he didn't hurry, but he didn't seem upset or worried by his friend's illness. He acted like he had everything under control. And, it turns out, he did.

When Jesus got to Martha and Mary's house, Lazarus had died. They had wrapped him in funeral wrappings and laid him in his tomb, which was a cave in the side of a rock. (*PUPPET COVERS HIS FACE WITH HIS HANDS.*) All of his friends had come there for his funeral, and everyone was extremely sad. But the saddest of all were Lazarus's sisters.

But they were mad, too. Why hadn't Jesus come earlier when Lazarus was still alive? They knew Jesus had the power to cure illness, but now that Lazarus had died, they figured there was nothing Jesus could do.

I think we act like Martha and Mary a lot. We want Jesus to come when we call, and we want him to do what we ask. We think we understand how God's power is shown in the world, what it can fix and what it sometimes can't. That can get in the way of building a relationship with God. Let's confess our sins together:

Prayer of Confession:
Loving God, we confess to you our low expectations about what you can do in our lives. We see so much of what's wrong in our lives and in our world as unchangeable. We doubt that you care. We find it hard to believe that things will ever be different.

Hear our confession, God, and put a new spirit in us. Help us to hear your invitation to new life, shouted loud and clear to us. Help us to notice all the places in our lives and in our world where you are at work, surprising us. Amen.

Narrator: After talking to Martha and Mary, Jesus went to Lazarus's tomb. When he saw all of the people there, crying because they missed their friend so much, Jesus started to cry too. That's how much he loved Lazarus.

But then he did something that surprised everyone there. To the people gathered around the tomb, he said:

Jesus: Take away the stone.

Narrator: Everyone was in shock. Lazarus had already been dead for days—did Jesus really want to look at his dead body? Wouldn't that just make everyone feel even worse?

But Jesus convinced them to do it. And then he stood at the opening of Lazarus's tomb and prayed. Then he did the most shocking thing of all. He put his head in the tomb and he yelled at the top of his lungs,

Jesus: LAZARUS! COME OUT!

Narrator: And lo and behold, Lazarus CAME OUT, still wrapped in the cloth he had been buried in. He was alive again! The people around him couldn't believe their eyes! But Jesus wouldn't let them just stand and stare. He had an instruction for all of the witnesses as well.

Jesus: Unbind him, and let him go.

Narrator: And they did. They unwrapped Lazarus, and suddenly he could move again. And move he did—JUMPING and DANCING and HUGGING EVERYONE.

Jesus showed all the people around that tomb that day something very important. He showed them that things that seem impossible for us are not impossible for God. He showed them that God is more powerful even than death—and that was something he was going to show them again on Easter.

But he showed them something else that day. He showed that everyone has a part to play in the new life that God invites us into. When we see God acting in the world in a surprising new way, we have a job to do. We need to unbind it and let it go—we need to make sure that we are open to surprises, to new life, to resurrection. Because, after all, when Lazarus came back to life it wasn't just good news for him. It was good news for his sisters, for his friends, for his whole town, and in fact, for the whole world! (*PUPPET REACHES ARMS OUT IN A WIDE GESTURE.*) Thanks be to God!

Changed and Challenged by Jesus
Week 6: Challenged in Jerusalem

Narrator: We've met some really great people over this Lenten season. Can you remember who came?

Nicodemus
The Woman at the Well
The Man Who Was Lame
The Man Born Blind
Lazarus

(*As each puppet is named by the children, they come out. They are wearing signs with their names on them.*)

Each of these people had a meeting with the same, very special person. Do you know who that was? (*Jesus.*) Right! And, through that meeting with Jesus, each of these people was changed in some way.

Nicodemus here thought he had to have all the answers to have a relationship with God. Even when he was confused (*PUPPET SPINS*), God loved him.

The Woman at the Well thought that she didn't matter, that no one would care for her. (*PUPPET SHAKES HER HEAD.*) When she met Jesus, she found out that God loves everybody. God's love is like a spring of water that never empties. It always has enough for all of us.

The Man Who Was Lame was stuck. (*PUPPET LIMPS AROUND IN A CIRCLE, WAVING HIS ARMS IN AN ANGRY WAY.*) But through meeting Jesus, not only was he healed of the problem with his leg but also the problem he was having in blaming other people.

The Man Born Blind got his sight from Jesus. (*PUPPET COVERS AND UNCOVERS HIS EYES.*) And what's more, Jesus helped him see the world in a new way, as a place where we can change, and invite others to change with us.

And last we have Lazarus here who was dead. (*PUPPET KNEELS DOWN AND COVERS HIS HEAD WITH HIS HANDS.*) Jesus surprised everyone by bringing him back to life. (*PUPPET STANDS AND WAVES HIS ARMS.*) Talk about a change!

Well, what I want to tell you about today is what happened after all these great meetings with Jesus. Today is Palm Sunday, the day we remember how Jesus rode into Jerusalem on a donkey. People were so excited that day. They crowded into the streets so that they could see Jesus riding in. Everybody came out to see it. And, you know what, I bet our friends here were there. They all knew Jesus and loved him and would have wanted to see him make his big entrance into Jerusalem. Like everyone else, I bet they were waving palm branches and shouting, "Hosanna! Hosanna!" (*PUPPETS ALL WAVE TOGETHER.*)

They must have been particularly excited because they knew who Jesus was—the Messiah, the Christ—and they knew that he had the power to change lives. After all, he had changed theirs!

But you know what, that is not the end of the story. (*ALL THE PUP-PETS LOOK AT EACH OTHER AND SHAKE THEIR HEADS.*)

After all the excitement of Palm Sunday, things got really hard. First, Jesus went into the temple and knocked over the tables of the people who were doing bad things there, and that made people angry. And Jesus was reminding people of how much they needed to change and how much they needed to love and people didn't want to hear it. (*PUPPETS PUT THEIR HANDS OVER THEIR EARS.*)

And, by the end of the week, on Friday, just five days after Jesus had ridden in on the donkey and people had shouted and waved their palms, what happened? That's right, Jesus was crucified.

And you know what? At that moment, when Jesus took his last breath and died, everybody thought that was the end of the story. And all the people who loved him thought that maybe he had been wrong. They thought that all the love he had shown them, and all the ways that he had changed them, didn't matter. They thought that death really was the end of the story.

I'll bet our friend Nicodemus thought that he must have answered all his questions wrong. I bet Nicodemus felt really DUMB. (*Someone flips over Nicodemus's name sign to show the word "Dumb."*)

And the Woman at the Well thought, with Jesus dead, God didn't really love her. She thought that she was, in fact, UNLOVABLE (*flip sign*).

And even though he could now walk, I'll bet our friend here thought he might as well be STUCK without Jesus (*flip sign*).

The man who used to be blind—even though he could see now—couldn't see love in the world without Jesus. He was back to being BLIND (*flip sign*).

And poor Lazarus. What was the use of living without Jesus? How could he have been brought back to life if the man who made it possible was now, himself, in a tomb? He might as well be DEAD (*flip sign*).

That is what it must have felt like for our friends on Good Friday when Jesus was crucified. I imagine that they all gazed silently at that cross on which their friend, Jesus, now hung, and thought that that was the end of the story. And so they left, heartbroken. (*PUPPETS WALK AWAY SILENTLY AS CONGREGATION PRAYS.*)

Friends, the story of Holy Week calls us all to examine our hearts, and to confess. Will you join me in our congregational confession.

Prayer of Confession:

Holy and gracious God, sometimes there are no words for our sorrow. It is hard to hear the story of the betrayal, the suffering, and the death of Jesus Christ. It is even harder to hear that story knowing that we still do not live the lives you call us to live. We still betray you. We still look for scapegoats. We still care more about our own safety than we care about justice or truth. Forgive us, God.

The story of Palm Sunday leads into Holy Week, but it doesn't end there. God does not abandon us, just as God did not abandon Jesus, even when Jesus cried out from the cross in despair. Death does not have the last word, and trusting in that, we can journey through this week, and through all of our dark times. There is light at the end of this long, dark tunnel. Come back next week to hear all about it!

Changed and Challenged by Jesus
Week 7: Changed by Easter!

Narrator: Happy Easter, everyone! We're here this morning because we're celebrating some really great news. Jesus is alive! Even though he died on a cross, even though he was buried, he didn't stay dead. God resurrected him! I think that's a reason to cheer, don't you? Let's have a big round of applause!

(*PUPPET ENTERS, BOWING AND WAVING.*) Well, hello! Look who we have here! Are you supposed to be Jesus? (*PUPPET SHAKES HIS HEAD NO AND POINTS TO HIS NAME TAG.*) Oh, wait. I think I know who you are. We've seen you here before. You're one of the people who met Jesus back when he was still alive, aren't you? (*PUPPET NODS AND JUMPS.*) Hey, can anyone remember his name? That's right— Nicodemus! (*PUPPET BOWS.*)

Nicodemus, I'm glad you're here, because you can help me tell the story of Easter. After all, you had a front row seat to everything that happened.

You all might remember that Nicodemus was a scholar of religion, someone who knew a lot about the Bible and worship and God's laws. He thought he understood God until he came to see Jesus one night. (*PUPPET MIMES KNOCKING ON A DOOR.*) Jesus told him that getting to know God wasn't just about reading and thinking and talking. To really get to know God, Jesus said, we have to get born all over again.

That confused Nicodemus terribly. (*PUPPET HOLDS HIS HEAD.*) How can you get born a second time? Jesus didn't really give him a straight answer, but he kept talking to Nicodemus. And the more Jesus talked, the more Nicodemus wanted this new birth, this new life that Jesus told him about.

Nicodemus continued to learn from Jesus, even after he left his house that night. (*PUPPET WALKS.*) We don't hear that much about him, though, until the end of the story. The Gospel of John says that after Jesus was crucified, Nicodemus and another man took Jesus' body and GENTLY PREPARED IT to be buried and laid it in a tomb.

Imagine his surprise, then, when he heard that Jesus' tomb was found empty the next day! (*PUPPET PUTS HIS HANDS OVER HIS MOUTH IN SURPRISE.*) Some people probably said that Jesus hadn't really been dead, that he had just been pretending. But Nicodemus knew that wasn't true, because he had held his dead body. So how could his tomb be empty? When the disciples starting saying that they had seen Jesus, I bet

Nicodemus remembered the conversation he had with Jesus that one night. (*PUPPET MAKES AN AHA! GESTURE.*) Maybe this was another example of what Jesus was talking about when he told Nicodemus about getting born all over again.

You know, Nicodemus never actually saw Jesus once he was resurrected from the dead. But I bet you he was one of the first ones to believe it happened. And what's more, I bet you he was one of the first ones to believe that resurrection wasn't just for Jesus. After all, Jesus had invited *him* into new life the first time he met him.

That's why Easter is such good news. It showed the world how God works, not just in Jesus' life, but in all our lives. God is always inviting us into new life. Even when we have given up hope for ourselves and for our world, God doesn't give up. Our God is a God of life and a God of birth and a God of hope.

Nicodemus, I know that wasn't always easy for you to understand. I know that when Jesus died, you probably doubted everything he had taught you. (*PUPPET NODS.*) Come to think of it, last week we even wrote a word on your name tag about how you felt when Jesus died. (*Turn tag over.*) You felt dumb. (*PUPPET HIDES HIS FACE IN SHAME.*) Well, you know what? You're not dumb! (*NARRATOR CROSSES OUT THE PUPPET'S SIGN.*) You were important to Jesus and I want to give you something to show that! Here's a new nametag for you. Can anyone read what it says? That's right—LOVED!

We're all loved—and that's what gives us the courage to open our hearts honestly to God. Will you join me in our congregational confession?

Prayer of Confession:
Mighty God, on this day of great celebration and praise, we open our hearts to you. Search us and know us. Forgive us our disbelief, our apathy, our cynicism, our anger, and our distrust. Open our hearts to the great, good news of this day. Help us to be not just those who hear that Christ is risen, but those who proclaim it. Amen.

Nicodemus, weren't there some other puppets besides you who visited us? I bet they would like to hear the good news of Jesus' resurrection too! I bet that's good news for their lives, too! Can you go find the other puppets and share the good news with them? The good news of Easter is too good to keep to ourselves! We are all born anew this day, forgiven and free! Thanks be to God!

COMMUNION LITURGIES

My (NWL) first call was as an associate minister in a church that had very traditional Communion services. On the first Sunday of the month, we would have all the parts of the usual service and then after the sermon and the second hymn we had our Communion service. Truth be told, the sacrament had a tacked-on quality to it. People were ready to go home, but there was this one other task we had to do—Communion.

The sacrament had about as much energy and excitement as the fourth quarter of football games when I was in high school. The Blackbirds would be behind forty-two to nothing; the visiting team had put in their second string. Our team's loss was a foregone conclusion, but we stayed in the stands through to the end out of loyalty. Years later, as I looked up from the Communion table to invite the congregation to enjoy "the gifts of God for the people of God," I could see on their faces the same bored looks that were on the faces of the fans in the stands of my high school team. Like them, we stayed in our places until the end. But our hearts and our minds had already checked out.

About six months into my ministry there, the youth group went on their annual winter hike up to a camp in the White Mountains of New Hampshire. I couldn't wait to go. I had heard lots of stories about the trips from years past, and I knew more or less what to expect. The culmination of the trip, I was told, was the tradition of waking up very early on the last morning up there, hiking out to Chapel Rock, and celebrating Communion as the sun rose. As their pastor it was up to me to plan this year's service.

We had a participatory, informal Communion service for that February morning. We celebrated the snow and the cold, the view of the mountains and the rocks beneath our feet, the Christian community we had in one another, and the presence of Christ in the bread and the juice. Our bodies and souls were alive with anticipation as we served one another the elements. Communion was not an addition to the rest of our worship; it was the peak experience of that worship.

It doesn't have to take a three-hour hike up through the snow to reach that pinnacle experience in worship. The sacrament itself can bring us spiritually to the mountaintop. What we need is to experience something that has become routine in a fresh way. Communion is not a place for change for change's sake; we don't make changes just to be different or creative. Every change that we make must be driven by our desire to encounter God more fully, listening to the Spirit to make thoughtful, creative, faithful changes that help open our eyes to the true gift that the sacrament is for us.

We recognize that it is a big step to tamper with something as sacred as Communion. Many of our churches have Communion sets that date back a century, inscribed with the names of the faithful. Some congregations have sung the same Communion hymn for decades. For this reason, some people argue that Communion should be one of the very last practices to change in worship, or that it should never be changed at all.

We disagree. The fact of the matter is that Communion, even in the most staid and traditional of churches, is interactive and participatory. It requires everyone in the congregation to respond in some way. It is an example of something that we do well, that we do right in worship—we have just stopped noticing what it is that we are doing.

We try to balance our desire for freshness with our respect for tradition in the Communion service by maintaining core pieces of the liturgy unchanged. For example, we always use traditional language for the words of institution. It is a humbling experience to repeat Jesus' words, "As often as you drink of this, do so in remembrance of me." Those words connect us, and our congregations, with a long, long line of Christians who have found in the Communion service a point of contact with the presence and power of Jesus Christ. We do not want to distract from that experience, but to highlight it. We have found that when we are flexible and creative in some parts of the Communion service while maintaining traditional language for the words of institution, those words actually stand out more than they do in a "regular" Communion service.

Start by Paying Attention to Communion as It Is Now

Before you even begin to change the Prayer of Thanksgiving or the Words of Invitation to the table, pay attention to what is already happening in your Communion service right now.

The first time I (NWL) led Communion at the church I now serve I was cautious about making changes. The church used a fairly traditional Communion service for a Congregational church. We served Communion in the pews with the little pieces of bread on the silver plates and the little glass cups in the special trays. After we together drank the juice from our little cups, people put their cups in the little cup holders in the pews. "Pock," "pock," "pock" rang through the sanctuary as the cups went into the holders. I smiled and said, "I just love that sound! When I hear that sound I experience it as a happy prayer of thanksgiving to God. Now with your voices, let us also lift up our thanksgiving to God with the unison Prayer of Thanksgiving in your Order of Worship."

After worship, several people, including a teen, told me how much they love that sound and how, for them, it is one of the things they love about Communion. By paying attention to what was already happening in the Communion service, the sensory experiences of sound, taste, and touch, we were able to begin to relax and be more receptive to participating in Communion rather than be passive observers of the ritual.

Notice the places in the Communion service where people are most engaged and active, the places where different sounds or movements are happening. Notice them and point them out to your congregation. Celebrate the texture of the bread that Anne makes at home in her oven. Point out the new tablecloth that Ginny has made for the Communion table and the color or the pattern that it adds to your worship space. As your congregation begins to see some of the variety that is already a part of Communion as you have it now, they will be more open to creating variety in other parts of the service.

Learning How to Come to God's Table

When we lived in Nicaragua we attended Mass at a small community church filled with old ladies and lots of little kids. One Sunday the priest preached to the congregation about how to receive Communion. In the endearing diminutive that I love in the Spanish language, he explained to the children how to hold their hands, where to look, and how to comport their bodies when they filed up to receive Communion. He recognized that Communion becomes more meaningful when we feel comfortable with the "how" of the sacrament. In our congregations, older members can be leaders of this kind of training. Several older members have told us that they learned as children how to pass the Communion plate and how to look their neighbor in the eye when serving them the bread or cup.

Don't forget the "why" of Communion, either. In a sermon, or even during the Communion liturgy itself, take time to lift up the meaning behind the way in which you partake of the sacrament. If you usually receive Communion in the pew, honor the ancient practice of Christians serving one another. Invite people to consider saying the name of the person to whom they are serving. If you usually receive Communion by coming forward to the front of the worship space, connect the act of coming forward with Jesus' call to us to become his disciples and follow him. Only when we begin to understand why we have "always done it that way" can we then begin to consider that there are other equally meaningful ways to participate in the sacrament.

Lay Leaders Are Essential

You can't do it alone. And, in most settings, pastors don't serve Communion alone; the deacons or some other lay leaders take part in the serving of Communion. These people can join you in modeling what Communion can be—they can serve you by looking you in the eyes, saying your name, and intentionally sharing the elements with you. They can also be teachers to the congregation, helping everyone to understand what the sacrament means and ways in which we can interact with the elements and with one another more intentionally and thoughtfully.

Give People the Chance to Celebrate Outside of Sunday Morning

Like many pastors, we have continuing education funds and a few weeks a year to go off to conferences or to retreat centers. As a result, we are pretty much guaranteed to experience Communion in small groups or in innovative worship several times a year. If we are lucky, we also celebrate Communion with youth at retreats or church lock-ins where play and spiritual practice are delightfully intermixed. Most people in the pews don't have such opportunities. Many people in our congregations have only ever experienced Communion in the sanctuary of their church, blessed by a minister in a robe and served by a deacon in a suit.

As one wise parishioner of mine once said, "We know what we know. We don't know what we don't know." We can find ways to celebrate the sacrament of Communion in different ways and in different settings so that others can have the experiences we have had. No one expects the antique silver Communion set to be brought out for a deacons' meeting, so why not celebrate Communion around the meeting table with cup and a plate from the church kitchen? If there are small groups that sometimes meet in homes in your congregation, why not go for a visit and serve Communion while you're there, sitting around a dining room table with a crusty loaf of bread from a neighborhood bakery? As you meet with couples who are preparing their wedding ceremonies, invite them to share Communion with you, and with each other, on your last session together. Use a simple chalice that will become your gift to them.

Places for Change

In what follows, we outline the four parts of the traditional Communion service and make suggestions and offer examples of ways that you can bring the mountaintop experience to your sanctuary. Root the ritual with some traditional words and phrases at its core. After that, go at your own pace or go nutty. God's creativity is abundant. "Come, for all things are now ready!"

Innovation in Invitations

The first step in moving your congregation from passive observers to active participants is in the invitation to Communion. If someone invites you to dinner and you want to go, you have to say "yes" to accept the invitation. The same is true with the Great Banquet God has given us.

But saying "yes" isn't always as easy as it sounds. Often barriers exist in our minds and hearts that make it hard for us to accept God's grace in our lives. We worry if God really had us in mind when God spread out the Great Banquet. We worry that what we have done or left undone prohibits our participation in the sacrament. In our Communion invitations we can explicitly address those barriers.

In the invitation, we can also evoke God's expansive vision and connect this moment with other places and other times. We can see how we, in our particular church in our particular time, are a part of God's salvation history. We are not observers to that history but participants in it.

In churches that have set liturgies where most of the Communion service will not or cannot vary, the invitation may be the place where you can do something different while you keep the rest of the liturgy the same. When you invite people to the table, you can step outside of what traditionally takes place and comment on what is about to happen so that people experience a liturgy they have known and loved for years in fresh and new ways.

Example 1: Address our underlying fears that we are not worthy to be at the table.

Leader: You are invited here. You were invited before you were even born, and you will be invited here if you grow up, if you go to college, if you change, if you move away.

You are invited here if you are old or if you're young, if you're gay or if you're straight, if you are poor or if you're rich, if you have faith or if you doubt.

Even when you die, our Scriptures promise that you will be invited to sit at God's table in heaven. You are invited here, to eat this bread and to drink from these cups, and by doing these things, to remember Jesus' promise that he will be with us always.

People: We accept the invitation!

Example 2: Make a clear connection to the theme that you have been engaging in during the rest of worship. (*This invitation was for a service centered on the book of Jonah.*)

No matter where in your life you are imprisoned, even if you feel consumed by enormous sin, come to this table. It is the table of liberation. At this meal, we find dry land—a way to steady our lives in the midst of rocky oceans, a place to stand. No matter who you are, no matter how lonely or lost or foreign you may feel, God's mercy is boundless and you can taste it and feel it here at this table. Here all hunger will be satiated. Here all thirst will be quenched. Come!

Example 3: Invite the whole world. (*Use this invitation on World Communion Sunday or throughout the year.*)

Leader: We are joined by Christians throughout the world at this table this morning.

In a small church in an Iowa town, devastated by drought and low grain prices, people gather at this table.

In an Iraqi village, amidst the rubble of buildings bombed and burned, people gather at this table.

(*Include these or other examples that refer to the concerns of the world that week.*)

In a grand cathedral in Rome, where those who gather feel dwarfed by the magnitude of the architecture, art, and history that surrounds them, people gather at this table.

In a storefront Pentecostal church in East Los Angeles filled with people from every country in Central America, people gather at this table.

In a tiny Japanese church, where all the parishioners know they have stepped outside of the mainstream of their culture, people gather at this table.

In a village in Kenya, where half the congregation is children and where only the oldest have a bench on which to sit, people gather at this table.

In an evangelical church in the heart of the American Bible Belt where people gather for morning and evening services that last several hours, people gather at this table.

In a tiny little urban church, with a dilapidated building and an elderly congregation, people gather at this table.

We have wonderful company, friends, in time and beyond time, for many have come to this table to know Christ in the breaking of the bread.

Example 4: Use examples from your congregation for the invitation.

Have people in your congregation share what Communion means to them. Make sure that everyone's voice gets heard by interviewing the deacons, different committees, the youth, and shut-ins. Listen to hear how God works in them through the sacrament. A friend interviewed some of the shut-ins in her congregation about their experience of Communion and they spoke of "renewal" and "healing." Use people's statements about Communion anonymously to craft Communion invitations that touch upon the varied and powerful meaning of the sacrament.

Innovation in Communion Prayers

The Communion prayer is a time when we connect the ritual act we are about to engage in with God's words and deeds throughout history. In our interactive Communion prayers, all worshipers raise their voices to praise God for God's glorious saving history and to proclaim our place in it.

Example 1: All Saints' Day, connecting our congregation with the saints, in time and beyond time.

Leader: We give you thanks, God of all times and places, for your unexpected and persistent involvement in the lives of our spiritual ancestors. These saving acts are made known to us through our scriptures and through our traditions, and especially through the life, death, and resurrection of Jesus, which stand at the heart of our common faith.

People: For the many saints of history who continue to uplift and inspire us today, we give you thanks.

Leader: You continue to reach out to us here and now, God of Love, creating us anew each day. For we are not bound by our history, but continually offered the opportunity to become a new creation in Christ. You sustain us when we are too weak to stand on our own, and offer us the blessings of your church, your community, your body on this earth.

People: For the many saints whom we encounter each day, we give you thanks.

Leader: Your promises to us do not end with this day, God of Glory, but draw us into the future. John the Evangelist has painted for us a vision of the day when all your saints will be united in heaven, singing praises to God and to the Lamb without ceasing. For the vision of this day, when our hearts and voices are united, and when our struggles cease, we give you thanks. Joining our voices with that celestial choir, we sing even now:

People: Holy, holy, holy! Lord God Almighty!

All thy works shall praise thy name in earth and sky
and sea;
Holy, holy, holy! Hosanna in the highest;
Blessed is Christ who comes to set us free!

Example 2: Connect ancient promises with our lives today. *(good for early Advent, or anytime)*

Leader: The story we have come to remember and celebrate today is the story of a promise, a promise splayed out in Noah's noonday sky, twinkling in the darkness of Abraham's starry night. Greeted with joyous laughter by Sarah, claimed in struggle by Jacob, dreamed of by Joseph, celebrated in dance by Miriam, this promise has been passed along by hand and mouth and heart.

Congregation: God is with us, God will guide us, God will not forsake us.

Leader: Jesus came as a fulfillment of that promise, and as an extension of it as well. When we saw Jesus in the manger, we saw how vulnerable God will become. When we saw Jesus on the road, we learned how strongly God will challenge us, how deeply God will heal us. When we saw Jesus on the cross, we discovered that there is nowhere God will not go to claim us; and when we saw the empty tomb, we fell to our knees and rejoiced, because we knew that God's promise is stronger than sin, stronger even than death.

Congregation: God is with us, God will guide us, God will not forsake us.

Leader: And so at this table, we claim that promise, eat it and drink it and make it our own. We are God's people, inheritors of an ancient promise, holding on fiercely as it pulls us forward into eternal life. Let us proclaim together the mystery of our faith:

Congregation: Christ has died, Christ is risen, Christ will come again.

Example 3: Make each part of the Communion prayer a charge to the congregation.

Leader: We give you thanks, O God, for the gift of your Son, Jesus Christ, our Lord. As we gather at your table, we charge ourselves to remember. We remember not only his birth in the stable and the adoration of shepherds, kings, and angels, but also the threat of death which hovered around him from the time he was born. We drove him out, from Bethlehem to Egypt, from Jerusalem to Golgotha. But on his way he left us this—the breaking of bread and the sharing of a cup passed among friends. Do this, he said, in remembrance of me.

Congregation: Help us, we pray, to remember and to proclaim the stories of our faith.

Leader: We give you thanks, O God, that death wasn't the end of the story. As we gather at your table, our hearts swell with joy. We celebrate Christ's resurrection and his promise to be with us always. We want to do something more than just remember a story of an evening at the end of Jesus' life. We want to experience the living Christ.

Congregation: Help us, we pray, to know Christ here and now, in the breaking and sharing of this bread.

Leader: We give you thanks, O God, that the story doesn't end with us. As we gather at your table, we anticipate the future. We trust that you guide us—guide our world—toward a time when there will no longer be many tables in many places, but one great table with room enough for us all. We are bold to anticipate the coming again of Christ, in time and beyond time.

Congregation: Help us, we pray, to be awake and watchful for signs of your coming.

Innovation in Sharing the Elements

There are many ways to add creativity and energy when you share the elements together. You can add variety in the manner in which people receive the bread and cup or you can vary the bread and what is in the cup. Here are a few suggestions:

- Vary the way in which Communion in your church is served. If you usually receive it in the pew, invite everyone to come forward one Sunday. If you usually receive it up front, have everyone stay seated. Try inviting people up to receive Communion in small groups. Have everyone gather around the Communion table (make sure to have many chalices and plates) and pass the elements around in a joyful, disorganized mix.
- If your polity allows it, vary who serves the bread and cup. Don't unseat your deacons permanently, but instead honor specific groups in your church by asking them to assist. Begin with the youth.
- Vary the places in the sanctuary from which it is served. Can you serve it at the baptismal font? At the back door where people leave to go out to the world?
- Vary the kind of bread you use. Be sure to include breads from different cultures and breads of different textures, sizes, and colors to reinforce and evoke the diverse expressions of the body of Christ.

Innovation in Prayers of Thanksgiving

Invite the congregation to sing a verse of a favorite hymn as the Prayer of Thanksgiving. Perhaps your congregation has a communal favorite hymn—their "song in the heart." The close of Communion is the perfect time to sing it. Another idea is to invite different members of the church to share their favorite hymns with the congregation. To take a really big step, invite those persons to give a short testimony about why they love the hymn they have chosen and how they have come to know Jesus through the song.

We have often concluded Communion with individual prayers of thanksgiving which are followed by a communal affirmation. Explain that all are welcome to share their prayers of joy and thanksgiving to God. After one person prays his or her prayer, invite everyone to proclaim, "Thanks be to God!" A happy word of warning: be prepared that *you* may be lifted up in thanksgiving to God.

Innovation in the Whole Liturgy

You've made changes to one part of the Communion service. Now you are ready to take the plunge with the whole liturgy. Here is an example of one such service. This Communion service could be used as a sermon and Communion service combined.

Example: Exodus theme

Leader:
"Then Moses and the Israelites sang this song to the LORD:

I will sing to the LORD, for he has triumphed gloriously;

horse and rider he has thrown into the sea.

The LORD is my strength and my might,

and he has become my salvation;

this is my God, and I will praise him,

my father's God, and I will exalt him." (Exodus 15:1-2)

"Then the prophet Miriam, Aaron's sister, took a tambourine in her hand; and all the women went out after her with tambourines and with dancing. And Miriam sang to them:

'Sing to the LORD, for he has triumphed gloriously;

horse and rider he has thrown into the sea.'" (Exodus 15:20-21)

The songs of Moses and of Miriam still echo today in our own songs of praise. God made the world! While all of the forces of the universe seek to disorder us and pull us apart, God triumphed over nothingness and made each of us. God gave us breath! And so with every breath we take we praise God, singing:

Congregation: Glory, glory, hallelujah!
Since I laid my burdens down.
Glory, glory, hallelujah!
Since I laid my burdens down.

Leader: The stories of our faith remind us that since creation began, God has reached out to us with saving power. God calls us out of bondage, releases us from all that holds us captive. With the gift of Jesus Christ, God continued that ancient story, assuring us that God continues to reach out to save us. Jesus was drawn from the water of the river Jordan and called out to the wilderness. Jesus challenged the rulers of his time, and called all people to follow him into freedom. Even the grave could not hold him captive. Each time we hear that story we cannot help but exclaim:

Congregation: Glory, glory, hallelujah!
Since I laid my burdens down.
Glory, glory, hallelujah!
Since I laid my burdens down.

Leader: God's story doesn't end with the Bible. It continues in our lives today. We have been blessed with water and called into the wilderness. We have been given the promise of freedom, and even though we yearn for the familiarity of captivity, God challenges us again and again to live into that promise. We have been called to challenge all that would oppress God's beloved people in our own day, and gifted and equipped for that purpose. Although we tremble at the call, we take strength knowing that the awesome power of God is with us:

Congregation: Glory, glory, hallelujah!
Since I laid my burdens down.
Glory, glory, hallelujah!
Since I laid my burdens down.

Leader: The life to which God calls us is not an easy one. While it leads us to the Promised Land, the land of milk and honey, it does so only by way of the desert. As we journey, we wonder at times if God has given up on us. And so we come, time and again, to this table. Just as God sustained the Israelites with manna, so are we sustained with these gifts of bread and cup. This is heavenly food for us, for here we remember that on Jesus' last night with his disciples, he gathered them at a table and shared a Passover meal with them. At that meal they told the story of God's saving acts in history. They told the story of Moses and Pharaoh and sang songs in celebration of his victory over death.

Congregation: Glory, glory, hallelujah!
Since I laid my burdens down.
Glory, glory, hallelujah!
Since I laid my burdens down.

Leader: And then, at the end of the meal, Jesus took the bread from the table and broke it, and gave it to his disciples, saying "This is my body which is broken for you. Do this in remembrance of me." And in the same way Jesus also took the cup after supper, saying: "This cup is the new covenant in my blood. Do this, as often as you drink of it, in remembrance of me."

Let us pray. Holy God, bless this bread and bless this cup. Fill them with your presence and your power, so that in sharing this meal with one another, we may remember your deeds, celebrate your presence, and anticipate the arrival of your kingdom. Amen.

Friends, when we share this bread and this cup with one another, we do remember. We remember the great stories of our faith. We remember Jesus. We remember the times that we have come to know firsthand God's saving power at work in our lives. And we remember our call to break free from all that would enslave us, to speak out on behalf of all who are oppressed, and to maintain our faith, even in the wilderness. These are the gifts of God for the people of God. Let us share the feast.

Music Heard and
Sung in New Ways

I (NWL) converted to Christianity at age twenty-seven. My baptism into Christ was many years in coming, but the seed of faith was planted in my soul when I was eight or nine years old and first saw the musical *Godspell*. I was raised in a secular/humanist household and wanted nothing to do with Christianity. But there, at that little summer stock theater production, when I watched Jesus share the Last Supper with his disciples as the band sang "On the Willows," I wept and almost dared to wish to be a follower too. When they carried Jesus' crucified body down the center aisle of the theater singing "Long Live God," quietly at first and then building gradually to a tremendous *forte*, I rejoiced that death did not have the last word in our lives and that resurrection was alive and at work in the world. I still couldn't believe God's Great Story with my head, but the music of God's salvational power had already begun to take hold of my heart.

We've seen it in our congregations again and again. People tell us that they find they can sing things well before they feel confident saying them. We don't see this as hypocrisy—we see it as training, as formation. Even if people are not sure that God loves and forgives them, singing "Amazing Grace" has an impact on their hearts that words alone do not. For one friend, it was our congregation's weekly repetition of the old hymn "Just As I Am" right after our Prayer of Confession that finally convinced him that he could be comfortable in a church community, even after years away.

We love music—but we're not professional musicians. We can sing adequately, we know the lyrics to just about every twentieth-century musical, and Heather can hold her own on the flute. We are quite clear, however, that we have not been called to our congregations to lead the choir, accompany the congregation's singing, or (God forbid!) perform a solo. But that does not mean that the music in worship is none of our business. We refuse to leave music to the professionals.

Here's the bottom line: we know that to get our whole congregation involved in worshiping God with their heart, soul, mind, and strength, we need to get our whole congregation participating in the music. That might mean singing well or it might mean singing poorly. It might mean clapping or moving to the beat or shaking a maraca or humming into a kazoo. Music in worship service cannot be simply a performance that is appreciated and listened to, while we stand at a distance from what is going on, observing and analyzing the quality of the performer. Why? Because music matters too much. It is one of the best ways to make the words and images and feelings and traditions of our faith move from our head to our heart.

Here are some suggestions and ideas for making music everyone's joyful work and not just the property of the choir, the organist, or the choir director.

Turn Performers into Worship Leaders

When it comes to negotiating changes in the music your congregation uses in worship, it is extremely important to have your priorities straight. Remember your goal: to improve people's experience of worship. With that goal in mind, the most important question is not what kind of music is performed and sung, but how music is being used, where, when, and to what effect.

We've known a number of ministers who have gone to battle with longstanding traditions of musical performance and longstanding music directors in their congregations. Almost all of them have lost. Knowing this, we've come to believe that worship leaders who want to make changes in the way in which music is used in their congregation's worship service can go about it one of two ways. We can either make the choir and the music director our teachers, our helpers, our guides, and our allies. Or, we can negotiate a truce and divide territory.

The first option is by far the best. After all, in most of our congregations, the choir consists of members of our congregation, and we are seeking to change their experience of worship as well. Build your relationship with choir members—don't let it be mediated entirely by the choir director. Take each member of the choir out to lunch, one by one, and ask about their experience of music. Affirm any connection they can make between music and spirituality, and remind them, over and over, that participation in the choir makes them worship leaders in your congregation. Their music can be a part of other people's spiritual journey as well as their own. As much as possible, have the same kind of conversations with any paid music leaders.

Then, ask the choir and music director for advice and assistance. Ask them to teach a refrain to the congregation that you'll later use during prayer, or at the end of a Communion service. Bring three possible response songs, and ask for their opinion about which one is best. Affirm, again and again, the important role they are playing in worship.

And then, ask them to do something other than perform an anthem. Ask them to introduce the worship theme (by singing at the start of worship). Ask them to introduce a scripture passage (by singing an anthem with the words of scripture directly before the sermon). Ask them to lead the congregation in prayer, or in thanksgiving, by singing together at a time in the service when those things are called for.

Each time they try something new, affirm them as *worship leaders*. Refer to them as such during worship. List them under that title in your bulletin.

Too often, the battles over music in congregations start because the minister, or some other group of worship leaders, wants to introduce new musical styles into the service. While we love a wide variety of music, we think that much of the debate over musical genre is a distraction. The central question is whether the music is leading the congregation in worship. We'd rather change the way in which the choir is singing familiar anthems first, and then nudge them toward trying new music later.

When All Else Fails, Divide Territory

We are aware that there are some congregations where the choir director is the one who is seated at the right hand of God, and he or she is simply unwilling to take a word of advice or direction from anyone else in the church. Clearly, such people do not see themselves as co-leading worship with you. They should be fired. But since that is not always a realistic option, many worship leaders simply need to work around them.

Find a couple of allies (preferably from the choir) and then sit down and have an honest conversation with the music director. Be respectful, but firm. You need some space to explore some new ways to connect worship and music. Could you have four Sundays a year as "music experiment" Sunday? One Sunday a month? Could you agree that the summer months will include a "musical experiment" each Sunday?

Or, consider starting a new worship service. A number of churches we know have had success with Sunday evening jazz services, or Saturday evening "contemporary" services with music led by a band. If every week is too daunting to begin with, just try it once. Or try it for Lent. Or for the summer.

Whatever you do, be sure to collect as much feedback as possible. Pass out surveys or interview participants, and report back to your deacons or worship team what you've learned. Don't just let the reactions and opinions of church leaders shape your decisions around music—focus on the feedback you receive from participants.

You may find allies in surprising places. At one church we knew, the music director and the choir were rumored to be dead-set against change. As we got to know the music director, however, we discovered that the music he led in church was not his preference at all. The committee who had hired him years before told him that the congregation strongly preferred classical music. Given permission by the worship leader, he was delighted to introduce some of his favorite gospel songs to the choir, and he did so with such enthusiasm and warmth that he quickly won everyone over.

To Everything There Is a Season

The Byrds and Ecclesiastes got it right; there is a right season for everything and that includes the introduction of new musical styles and instruments in worship. Choose your time wisely. For example, we have found that summertime is a great season for singing new and different kinds of music. People are more relaxed at that time of year. Even churches with very formal worship styles tend toward more informality when the days get hot and balmy. Seize the season as a time for some experimentation in music.

By the same token, there is also a season not to make changes. The biggest of these is Advent and Christmas. Don't mess with "Silent Night" or "Joy to the World." From a tactical standpoint, people simply will *not* follow you on that one. But more important, people are already engaging fully in these carols.

With this overall strategy in mind, here are some places to begin:

Hymn Sings

Many of the older members of our congregations grew up with the tradition of hymn sings and know the power of sitting in a group and singing old favorites with harmony and feeling. Affirm that wonderful Christian pastime and find ways to incorporate it into your worship. In one church we know, every fourth Sunday is congregational choice for hymns. People can't wait to raise their hands and call out their favorite hymns. A variation on that idea is asking worshipers to write down their favorite hymns and then picking them out of a hat and singing them throughout the worship service. Some Sunday, skip the sermon entirely and proclaim your faith in song.

To make a hymn-sing Sunday even more meaningful, invite people to say a short one-or two-sentence testimony about what the hymn they have chosen means for them. Ask them to share where they first learned or heard the song, or what their favorite line is and why. These stories are among the easiest ways we have to share the story of our faith with each other, and you may find that people who are normally unwilling to speak personally about their faith can do so in this way.

Get Instrumental

A great way to liven up our music is to add instrumentation. You might be lucky enough to have a clarinetist or trombonist or saxophone player in your congregation who could add an instrumental verse to a favorite hymn. Or, pass out a basket of rhythm instruments—tambourines, maracas, shake-a-eggs. If anyone objects, just explain that it's "for the children"—and then be sure to give that person the bongo drums that week!

On special occasions, why not try a kazoo choir? There is just about nothing better for "When the Saints Go Marching In" on All Saints Day or the Sunday before Lent (and Mardi Gras). You can order a gross of plastic kazoos from party supply catalogues for very little money. Be sure that adults, as well as kids, get one. And be sure to include at least one "all kazoo" verse!

Worship Around a Particular Style of Music

A few years ago *O Brother, Where Art Thou?* introduced old-time Americana music back into the American mainstream. All of a sudden, everyone was snapping up bluegrass music and enjoying that rich

American musical tradition; the people in our churches were no exception. Of course, much of the music on the *O Brother, Where Art Thou?* soundtrack in particular and bluegrass in general is about Jesus. We decided to create a worship service around the music of the movie. Heather got talented members of her congregation to learn the music and lead the congregation in worship on several occasions, including a "Bluegrass Christmas" service. (There's no better accompaniment to "Silent Night" than the banjo!) Nancy's church hired a local contra dance band to play the music throughout the service, and a small women's group formed to lead the congregation in a few a cappella songs.

Having a "theme" like this for a Sunday's music not only makes that service a special attraction, but it also provides an excuse to suspend the rules that normally order your worship service. Not only can you sing different songs, but you can also use music in different places in the service. Invite a guest musician to lead you in a jazz service, or a gospel service. Beatles Sunday is an annual hit at Heather's congregation ("Here Comes the Sun," "Let It Be," and "All You Need Is Love" fit nicely into the service). What might be a particular draw for your congregation? What might showcase the musical talents of your members?

If You Can Talk, You Can Sing

A Zimbabwean proverb says, "If you can talk, you can sing." If there are times when your congregation speaks in unison, consider replacing the spoken word with song. For example:

- Sing a verse of a hymn as an invitation and welcome as a family or individual comes forward to participate in the sacrament of baptism. Sing another verse as a celebration of the baptism. Try "Glory, Glory, Hallelujah!" or "I Was There To Hear Your Borning Cry." Or, ask the family if they have a favorite hymn. One Sunday, we sang "What a Wonderful World" as a request as a family walked through the congregation with their newly-baptized daughter. There wasn't a dry eye in the house.
- After announcing our forgiveness in Christ, sometimes we just feel like singing. Why not? Just make sure the song is one of gratitude.
- A simple sung refrain can be a beautiful blessing of the elements of Communion.

- Try singing the Lord's Prayer some weeks instead of saying it. Don't just let your soloist perform it, either!
- Music also makes a beautiful benediction. Try one verse of "God Be With You Till We Meet Again" or "Dona Nobis Pacem."

Exodus Lessons and Carols

One way to open up your congregation's experience both of music and of scripture is to tell a Bible story using songs as well as readings. What follows is just one example of a Bible story told in this format, **Exodus Lessons and Carols**. In this service, we tell the story of Moses and the Israelites in Egypt through song, story, and interaction with the congregation. We have found that children and adults learn the Bible story in a new way (or for the very first time) when we use this technique of blending music and story in worship. This is a great piece to use as a sermon in an intergenerational service.

Once you've told the Exodus story in song, story, and congregational response, consider other stories that can be brought to life when music, story, and faithful interaction combine. The prodigal son, Noah's ark, Joseph and his brothers, Daniel in the lion's den—just about any story— can be told this way.

Exodus Lessons and Carols

Materials

- 11 pieces of standard 2 feet-by-3 feet white poster board.
- Big black marker.

Preparation

- Write out all of the sound effects on the poster board. (You can and should use both sides of the poster board). Make sure that you have written largely and boldly enough so that the words can be seen from the back of your worship space.
- Find youth—at least three—to be the sound effects people for the service. They will jump at the chance! Have a short rehearsal with them (ten minutes) to make sure that they understand the concept and are ready to go.
- It is likely that not all of the songs for this service will be in your hymnbook. Make sure that a few weeks before this service you find all of the songs you need. Check in with your music leaders to see if they have the music. Check out the web. Bear in mind that you may have to order a few pieces.
- Give the service to your music leaders ahead of time so that they understand how the service will work and can prepare for the cues for the music.

Things to Consider

- This kind of service may seem new to most, if not all, the people in your congregation. Remind them that, at Christmas, we Christians often have a Lessons and Carols service to tell the Nativity story. You are using the same model for this service. When you put it in that context, people are going to feel much more open to the experience and it won't appear quite so different.

The Exodus Story

We're going to tell a story today about a man who lived a long, long time ago. I imagine many of you have heard of this man. His name was Moses. Have you heard of him? (*Nods.*) I said, have you heard of Moses? (*Yes!*) I guess before I go any further I need to explain something. I'm not going to tell this story to you—you're going to tell it with me. For one thing, we're going to tell the story with songs, some of which we'll sing together. For another thing, we're going to tell the story with a few sound effects.

You see, the story of Moses is a very exciting story; and in my experience, all the most exciting stories come with sound effects. You know, WHOOSH and OUCH and SPLAT and stuff like that. Now, since we don't have the help of all the equipment they use to make these sounds for major motion pictures, we'll have to make them ourselves. Are you game? We'll keep it simple—when you see one of the teens near me holding up a sign, you just have to make the sound that's indicated there. Let's give it a try:

(*WHOOSH, OUCH, SPLAT.*) Wow, that's great! There'll be some other sounds too, but I think you've got the hang of it.

So, here's the story. Moses was born in Egypt a long, long time ago—back before Jesus was born, back when the Pharaoh ruled. Moses was born in Egypt, but he was not Egyptian. Moses was an Israelite, which means that he was part of a group of people that had moved to Egypt from Israel. They had moved there several generations before Moses was born because there was a famine in Israel and there was food in Egypt. But by the time Moses came around, the Israelites (*Moses' people*) had become slaves to the Egyptians. Do you know what slaves are? They are people who have to work for someone else, whether they want to or not. And they don't get paid for their work. And, if they don't work hard, they get punished. Badly.

(*OUCH.*)

As if that wasn't bad enough, when Moses was born, it was actually against the law in Egypt for an Israelite to have a boy baby. But Moses' mother loved him, and so she came up with a plan to save his life. She put him in a basket, and hid the basket in the reeds on the side of the Nile River. She hid him in a place where she knew he would be discovered by the princess of Egypt, Pharaoh's daughter. And when the Pharaoh's daughter heard baby Moses cry, (*WAHHH!*) she loved him, and decided to adopt him as her own son. And she gave him the name "Moses," which means "to draw out," because she drew him out of the water. Little did she know that he would grow up to be the one whom God called to draw the Israelites out of their slavery in Egypt and into the Promised Land.

SONG: *"WHEN ISRAEL WAS IN EGYPT'S LAND"*

Moses grew up as part of the Egyptian royal court, but he never forgot that he was an Israelite. And things weren't great for the Israelites in Egypt. They had to work extremely hard making bricks, and then using the bricks to build buildings and roads all throughout Egypt. It was exhausting work, but if they ever got tired or slowed down, you know what happened, right?

(Teen on one side holds up sign.) (OUCH!)

One day, Moses saw an Egyptian beating an Israelite slave, and he couldn't take it any longer. He knew it wasn't right, and in a fit of rage, he jumped in and hit the Egyptian back.

(Teen on the other side holds up sign.) (WHAM!)

And he killed him! When he realized what he had done, he panicked; and he ran away before he could get in trouble. He ran so far that he ran to another country called Midian. And when he got there, he decided to stay. He ended up getting married, having some children, and becoming a shepherd. He figured that's what he'd probably do for the rest of his life.

But God had other plans for him. One day, Moses was out tending his sheep when he saw a bush that was on fire.

(Two teens hold up signs.) (SIZZLE! CRACKLE!)

When he looked closely, he realized that although the bush was in flames, it wasn't actually getting burnt up at all. And then, Moses heard the voice of God calling to him from the bush: "Moses! You are on holy ground!" the voice said. "I have heard the cries of my people who are suffering in Egypt. I will free the Israelites, Moses, but I need you to go and bring them out of Egypt."

When Moses got over his shock, he did what I imagine most of us would do in that situation: he tried to find an excuse that would get him out of the job. He said he wasn't a good public speaker; he said no one would believe him that he was sent by God. But God wouldn't accept any of Moses' excuses, and eventually Moses did what God told him. He went back to Egypt to confront the Pharaoh, and to tell him to let the Israelite people go free.

SONG: *"PHARAOH, PHARAOH"*

Well, Moses knew he was on a special mission from God, and when he first got to Egypt he had a lot of confidence. He went right up to see the Pharaoh, and he told him straight out: "Let my people go!" And what do you think Pharaoh said?

(*NO!*)

Not only did Pharaoh not do what Moses asked, he actually did the opposite. He made the Israelites work even harder, and he made their punishments even more severe.

(*OUCH!*)

But God wasn't about to give up, and God wouldn't let Moses give up either. God sent him right back in to talk to Pharaoh again. "Let my people go!" Pharaoh said the same thing he did before.

(*NO!*)

But this time, God gave Moses some special powers to help convince him. When Moses struck the Nile River with his staff, the whole river turned into blood.

(*EW! GROSS!*)

And as if that wasn't bad enough, God sent hundreds of thousands of frogs to hop all over Egypt.

(*RIBBIT! EW! GROSS!*)

Well, that grossed the Pharaoh out so much that he told Moses the Israelites could leave as soon as all the frogs died. But when the frogs died, he changed his mind. And when Moses asked him to free the Israelite slaves, Pharaoh said . . .

(*NO!*)

It went on like this for a long time. God would make something really bad happen in Egypt, Pharaoh would promise to free the slaves, the bad thing would go away, and then Pharaoh would change his mind. And there were a LOT of bad things that happened. There were lice.

(*SCRATCH! SCRATCH!*)

There were flies.

(*BZZZZ! BZZZZ!*)

There was a disease that killed all the cattle.

(*MOO! OUCH!*)

There was a horrible disease that gave everyone spots.

(*EW! GROSS!*)

There was hail.

(*BAM! BAM!*)

There was a grasshopper invasion that ate all the crops up.

(*MUNCH! MUNCH!*)

And then there were three days when the sun didn't come up.

(*WHO TURNED OFF THE LIGHTS?*)

And then finally, there was the worst plague of all. One night, all the first-born children of the Egyptian families died. But the children of the Israelites were spared. When Pharaoh realized what had happened, he finally had had enough. He called Moses to him and commanded him to leave at once, and to take every single Israelite with him. He didn't want to keep the Israelites as his slaves anymore. The Israelites packed up quickly and set off to leave Egypt. They looked forward to living as free people in a free land. But first, they had to cross the Red Sea. And that's where the story gets really amazing.

SONG: "WADE IN THE WATER"

When the Israelites got to the Red Sea, they realized they were in trouble. They looked behind them and saw Pharaoh's army coming after them! Just like he had done so many times before, Pharaoh had changed his mind, and he wanted to bring the Isrealites back to Egypt. Well, do you think God was going to let that happen?

(NO!)

That's right. And so God gave Moses the power to perform a miracle. Moses raised his arms, and the waters of the Red Sea parted in two, and there was a path of dry land right down the middle.

(WHOOOSH!)

And the Israelites could walk right on through without even getting their feet wet! But when the Egyptian soldiers started across that same dry path, right on the heels of the escaping Israelites, Moses raised his arms again and the waters closed back over the path; and all the Egyptian soldiers were drowned.

(WHOOOSH! SPLAT!)

When the Israelites realized what had happened, they knew that they were finally free. They knew that nothing would ever bring them back into slavery. They knew they could finally live the kind of life that God intends everyone to live—a life of freedom, a life of possibility, a life free from abuse and assault, a life lived in gratitude to God.

And do you know what the first thing they did in their new life was? They sang a song. Moses' sister Miriam led them, playing the tambourine and dancing along with all of the other women. And maybe their song sounded something like this:

SONG: "O FREEDOM!"

SPECIAL SERVICES

Sometimes You Have to Break the Mold Completely

The thing about changing your Sunday morning worship service is that most of your congregation knows what's "normal." They know the way it's supposed to go, and even if they go along with trying things a new way one Sunday, they are very aware of the change because they are so familiar with the previous practice.

If you really want to try out some new practices in worship, start off on a special occasion.

Mind you, we don't mean Christmas Eve. Don't try anything innovative that night. Just let people sit in their pews with their families and their candles and sing "Silent Night." But what about New Year's Eve? What about Twelfth Night? What about the Sunday before a new school year starts? Our year is filled with special days, religious and secular, some that we celebrate at home, others that go by unnoticed. Why not make one of those a special occasion for worship at your church?

Let everyone know that special days require special behavior. If someone asks why a bolt of blue cloth is spread down the center aisle of the church, patiently explain that today you are celebrating All Saints' Day and leave it at that. You may find, as we have, that your worship attendance is higher on these "Special Sundays," and people start coming to those events especially open to the Spirit moving in their lives.

It All Started with Ash Wednesday

In the Presbyterian Church where I (HKD) grew up, we didn't have an Ash Wednesday service. That sort of thing was considered "too Catholic" for Presbyterians—an opinion that was reinforced for me quite firmly by my mother. The idea of walking around with a smudge of ash on your forehead violated her sense that piety should not be shown in public.

When I was twelve, our church hired a new minister, and he instituted an Ash Wednesday service. It came as a surprise to my family. We went to church one evening for the annual Shrove Tuesday Pancake Dinner sponsored by the youth group—a fun event with balloons and streamers and lots of kids whizzing around on a sugar high. As the meal was coming to a close, the minister stood up on the stage in the church hall and started talking about beginning our Lenten Journey. One thing led to another. His comments about sin led to an invitation to repent of our sins; and before we knew what was coming, he had a bowl of ashes and was inviting everyone who wanted to come up to the stage to be marked with the sign of the cross.

I was intrigued. It all seemed to be part of the fun of the night, and I sprung to my feet and started heading to the stage. I didn't get far before my mother's firm grip on my arm returned me to my seat. "Stay seated!" she hissed into my ear. She didn't need to explain further. I understood her message a lot more clearly than I understood the minister's invitation, after all.

When I became a pastor, I still considered myself fairly inexperienced in the ways of Ash Wednesday. To be honest, my mother's prohibition still rang in my ears. What was the occasion all about, anyway? I read up on sin (always a fun way to spend a week), and was struck by all the ways the Bible talks about it, and all the ways we think about it these days. Could there really be just one word for such a complex idea?

I started crafting a sermon for Ash Wednesday that explored a number of metaphors for sin and repentance. The sermon became longer and longer. I briefly considered writing an eight-part sermon series on sin, but abandoned that idea when I considered what such a series might do for worship attendance.

So I decided to take a risk. I stepped "out of the box" of a traditional Ash Wednesday service entirely. Instead of rows of chairs, I set up tables in my chapel, and clustered chairs around them. I hired a cellist, and invited people as they entered the worship space to use the next thirty minutes to explore the tables with the help of a booklet with scripture and instructions.

Just to be sure all my bases were covered, I followed the thirty minutes of open time with a short Ash Wednesday Vespers service that I took straight out of my denomination's Book of Worship. The service worked—for me and for my congregation—and we repeated it with elaborations for many years. (You can try it too—it's outlined in this book!)

Mind you, not everyone participated in the interactive part of the service. There were always a few people each year who, for whatever reason, preferred to find a seat off to the side and spend the time sitting quietly, listening to the cello music. The service succeeded in large part because the invitation was so open. Each table held an invitation to consider sin and forgiveness in a different way. If a particular image didn't "click," the invitation was clearly to move on and explore a different one. This expansive invitation was powerful enough that it overcame all of the internal barriers we brought to the service.

Mine Your Tradition for Interactive Worship

Like Ash Wednesday, there are other Christian traditions that bear repeating. On the CD, you'll find suggestions for special services for All Saints' Day and Burying the Alleluia. Both are ancient traditions in the historic Christian church, but they were never practiced in our congregations until recently. When the occasional complaint is still made adopting "Catholic" practices, we try to remind our congregation that the Protestant and Catholic churches were at one time the same church, and these ancient Christian practices are part of our shared heritage. The same thing goes for Blessing the Animals on St. Francis' Day or House Blessings or Easter Vigils, all wonderful occasions for interactive worship.

If we want our experience of worship to be less superficial, sometimes it helps to engage in practices that have deep, deep roots in our history and heritage.

Don't Be Afraid to Ritualize Secular Traditions

Bless the local racetrack or the Little League diamond on opening day. Have a special service of recognition for the kindergartners who are starting their formal education. Have your whole congregation pray over the sixteen-year-old who has just gotten her driver's license. And by all means, bless all the women (not only those who are biologically mothers) on Mother's Day and all the men on Father's Day. If you live in a farming community, bless the harvest. If you live in Florida, bless the community at the start of hurricane season. These are big events in the life of our community, and when we make a connection between them and religious ritual, we increase the chance that we'll integrate our faith with the rest of our lives.

Make the Participants the Leaders

The temptation will always exist to make an occasion "sacred" simply by having a clergyperson say a prayer, preferably while wearing a robe and stole, or at least a clerical collar. Avoid this temptation at all costs! The role of clergy is to facilitate, to coach leaders, and to assist in leadership, but not to "perform" the rituals themselves.

Make sure other people pray. If they are too shy, ask them to write their prayer requests down, and read them out loud. Ask them to say a word about their dreams or their fears. Invite them to read a favorite scripture out loud. Share a drawing by each kindergartner. Let the older mothers give special blessings to the new mothers in the community.

Don't Forget to Decorate

Good worship is multisensory, and special occasions can give us all the excuse we need to add new colors and textures to our worship spaces. A few ideas to consider:

- A couple of yards of fabric laid across your altar or Communion table is an inexpensive way to introduce a color or a pattern to the worship space. A lot of fabric (which can still be pretty inexpensive if you look for remnants) can make a dramatic impact. Wrap your pulpit up in an African patterned cloth for African American History Month. Drape the choir loft with a dramatic red for Pentecost. No sewing required!
- On World Communion Sunday, or another Sunday with an international focus, invite members of the congregation to bring in any cloth (tablecloths, runners, scarves, shawls) they might have that comes from a different country. Layer them on the Communion

table and drape them anywhere you can in your chancel. You might be surprised what people have in their closets!

- White Christmas tree lights are a magical addition to any evening worship service, whether or not it's during Advent.

- Discount stores often sell the bright, seasonal banners that people hang outside their houses. One of these in the sanctuary might look a bit too cute, but ten of them start to make an impact. Try them for Easter, or to celebrate the church's birthday.

- Brightly colored kites are another inexpensive, high-impact addition. Try them on Pentecost, and preach about the wind of the Holy Spirit keeping us aloft.

Opportunities for Interactive Worship Are Everywhere

We've included several resources for special services for your use. You will find in print and on the CD an interactive **Ash Wednesday Service**, which we think is a great place to start. On the CD you will find other resources for just about every season of the church year—**A Longest Night Service** to be used on December 21, the longest night of the year; **Burying the Alleluia**, resources and ideas for the start of Lent; **Maundy Thursday Monologues** for that holy night; and an **All Saints' Day Liturgy** that people within our congregations have loved.

And, once your congregation has gotten behind the idea that special occasions require special worship, you'll have no end of reasons to worship. Just be sure that each and every service includes and involves the congregation in leadership. With good coaching, you may not even need to attend. Here are just a few suggestions:

- The night before your youth group leaves for their mission trip, invite the group along with their parents, families, friends, and the entire congregation to a special commissioning service at the church. Each participant might share a hope and a fear for the week to come, and parents might offer a special blessing. Then invite the whole community to gather around the teens and pray over them with a traditional "laying on of hands." We once had a ritual at the end of such a worship service in which the youth ran through all the outstretched hands of the congregation like football players do right before a game. Everyone felt a part of the action and the youth really understood that they were players on a whole team and that the work they were about to do was on behalf of a much larger group of people who would be praying for them.

- Bless your church's rummage sale right before it opens. This can be sacred and silly at the same time—invite everyone to hold (or wear!) the ugliest item they can find while you all pray together for every person who will step into your church yard or building that day.
- Have a special service for anyone being deployed by the military before he or she leaves.
- By all means bless the animals, around St. Francis' Day or any other time of year.
- Why not hold a "blessing of crochet hooks" some morning with the Ladies' Circle as they prepare to make baby blankets for the local hospital or prayer shawls for a hospice program? Or bless the workers as they assemble health kits for Church World Service. If your congregation works on a Habitat for Humanity house or collects food for the food pantry, develop a short worship service blessing those who benefit from your efforts. Do it on site if at all possible, and include staff or others on site. Find ways to relate the mission activity of the congregation to its worship life.

You and your congregation are doing somersaults in the water now! You are ready for the deep end.

Ash Wednesday Interactive Service

Introduction

This is the service that started me (HKD) on the journey. It has become my standard for a service that balances innovation and tradition, introspection and corporate reflection, new twists with ancient roots. After taking part in his first interactive Ash Wednesday service, one man wrote me, "That service, with all its metaphors and images, is actually a good allegory for what a life of faith ought to be—that is to say, personalized prayer and reflection coupled with a supportive joining together in community."

Materials

Now is the time to raid the supply closet for this service. Here is what you will need:

Stiff/Made Soft
- Malleable clay.

Missing the Mark/Re-aiming
- Dart boards (at least 2).
- Darts.

Stained/Made Clean
- Markers.
- Stones. Collect them on a calming Ash Wednesday prayer walk or buy them at a store like Bed, Bath, and Beyond.
- Small water fountain. If you don't own a fountain, ask around and you will probably find that someone you know has one. If not, you can buy one at a home decorating store like Target or Bed, Bath, and Beyond.

Holding Tight/Letting Go
- Vase that you can put your hand into.
- Candies at the bottom of the vase.

Release/Re-creation
Nothing!

Contaminated/Purified
- Slips of paper.
- Candle.
- Metal bowl. Avoid using a special family heirloom as people will put burning paper into this.

Built on Sand/Built on Rock
- Sand.
- Rocks (more rocks from your prayer walk).
- 2 buckets.

Futility/Fertility
- Flower seeds.
- Potting soil.
- Paper potting pots.

Casting Stones/Laying Our Stones Down
- More stones.
- One large bowl.
- Several small bowls.

Preparation

- A few days ahead of time, create an Ash Wednesday booklet. The booklet should include an introduction (sample included in this book) and a page for each station you plan to use for the service. Make sure that each booklet contains space for people to include their reflections on the stations. Also include an Order of Worship for the Vespers service you will have after the stations time.
- Copy the booklet so that you have enough for all participants.
- Select a worship space. If you have a chapel in your church, perfect. If not, find a room in your church where you can set up a few rows of chairs in "traditional" worship formation and still have room for the interactive stations made up of tables and chairs.
- Select the interactive stations that will be a part of your service; we have included eight stations for your consideration. Due to the size

of the room and the number of people participating, we have used four stations in the services we have led. Tailor the number of stations to fit your context.

- Set up for the service. In one half of the room, have a communal worship space with a few rows of chairs near the piano. In the other half of the room, set up a table for each station you will use and then place all the items you need on each table. Place a few chairs around each table so that at least two people can interact with the station at a time. Make sure that you have enough supplies at each table so that several people can use the station. (This service takes a couple of hours to set up. Factor that into your planning for the day and get help.)
- Ensure you have background music. People will be much more comfortable engaging in the stations if soothing music plays in the background. If you can have live music, great. If not, find good, calming, instrumental music to play on your iPod or CD player.

Things to Consider

- The first time you use this service will be a new experience for everyone. Make sure that you take the time to welcome people at the beginning of the service and explain what will happen. Answer any questions people might have about the process and let them know how long they will have to explore the stations. We know that this service will become a favorite in your church. After the first year, many people will already know what to expect when they come to the service. But, for the first year, make sure that you help people along in the process and give them clear expectations so they feel at ease.
- If your worship space does not lend itself to the stations format, consider creating an Ash Wednesday service around one of the stations we have included. You could have a traditional Ash Wednesday Vespers service but add in an interactive component.
- Some people think best by talking. After you have allowed for introspection, perhaps people would like to share their experience with another person. Consider having a one-on-one sharing time after people have been around to the different stations. To get the conversation rolling between people, you might ask, "Which station felt most comfortable?" "Which station touched you most deeply?" "Did

you skip a station? Why?" "How did your understanding of sin change through this experience?"

- This service is very accessible to children. As you publicize this service, make sure that you explicitly invite children and let their parents know that this is an experiential service that kids will enjoy. If you are in a congregation with many children and families and are concerned about space, consider having two services, one for families and one for adults. In all cases, invite young children to pair with adults as they visit the stations so that the adults can read instructions and explain the activities.

Ash Wednesday Booklet Introduction

At the start of a journey...

Welcome to Ash Wednesday worship at _____. We will begin our worship service this evening with a period of individual reflection, guided by different "stations" with an image and activity. You may wish to visit only one table, or all of them. Or, you may simply wish to take time to sit quietly with your own thoughts, listening to the musical meditations.

Traditionally, the Lenten journey begins with confession on Ash Wednesday. As we prepare to journey toward a closer relationship with God, we need to step back and consider the ways in which we have put distance between ourselves and God.

Each of the tables in our chapel tonight suggests another image or metaphor for sin and forgiveness. Separation is one way to understand sin; reunion is one way to understand forgiveness. But there are a hundred other ways as well, and each might strike us differently at different times.

There is space at the bottom of each page where you might wish to jot down some thoughts. If you don't feel you are ready to write anything now, you might save this booklet and use it later. Or you might want to return to what you write tonight at some later point during Lent, continuing your reflections and prayers.

At the end of approximately twenty minutes, we will gather together for a short Vespers service, adding our corporate confession to our individual reflections. You will find an Order of Worship for this service at the end of this booklet.

Stiff/Made Soft

Yet, O LORD, you are our Father;
    we are the clay, and you are our potter;
    we are all the work of your hand. (Isaiah 64:8)

The word that came to Jeremiah from the LORD: "Come, go down to the potter's house, and there I will let you hear my words." So I went down to the potter's house, and there he was working at his wheel. The vessel he was making of clay was spoiled in the potter's hand, and he reworked it into another vessel, as seemed good to him.

Then the word of the LORD came to me: Can I not do with you, O house of Israel, just as this potter has done? says the LORD. Just like the clay in the potter's hand, so are you in my hand, O house of Israel. (Jeremiah 18:1-6)

Reflection: One of the ways in which sin is described in the Bible is as a "hardness of heart." Do you ever feel that your heart is hard, that it is inflexible, or judgmental? Do you find that your compassion for others is limited? Do you keep your guard up in your relationships with others and/or with God? Reflect on the ways in which this is true.

Action: Take a piece of clay. Warm it in your hands and knead it until it becomes pliable. Shape it into something new. As you shape the clay, imagine God shaping you in the same way.

Missing the Mark/Re-aiming

Since all have sinned and fall short of the glory of God; they are now justified by his grace as a gift, through the redemption that is in Christ Jesus. (Romans 3:23-24)

Reflection: The Greek verb for sin used in many places in the New Testament is *hamartano*, meaning, "to miss the mark." If we think of "the mark" as God's will and way for us, then perhaps we miss when we aim for something else (like success, perhaps, or wealth). Or perhaps we just don't shoot with enough energy and "fall short," as Paul suggests in Romans. How does this image fit with your understanding of sin in your own life and in the life of our community?

Action: Don't throw the darts! Just take one from the outside of the board and redirect it to the bull's eye. Do so with some reflection about how you might redirect your own life so that you are more "on target."

Stained/Made Clean

Create in me a clean heart, O God,
   and put a new and right spirit within me.
Do not cast me away from your presence,
   and do not take your holy spirit from me.
Restore to me the joy of your salvation,
   and sustain in me a willing spirit. (Psalm 51:10-12)

Reflection: One of the most ancient metaphors for sin is dirt. And while this image has its limits, it certainly has its strengths as well. Part of what pulls us away from God, after all, is our involvement with things that are ungodly. "Woe is me!" Isaiah cries when he is brought before the throne of God, "I am lost for I am a man of unclean lips, and I live among a people of unclean lips!" Just as a child has to get washed up before coming to the dinner table, so must we cleanse ourselves of all that drags us down in the world as we begin to approach God.

Action: Using one of the markers on the table in front of you, draw a dot on one of the small rocks. As you do so, you might wish to give that dot the name of a sin that you would like to confess to God. Put the rock into the fountain on the table and watch it be made clean, knowing that God's forgiveness also cleanses you.

You may wish to take the clean stone with you as a reminder, or you may leave it in the fountain.

Holding Tight/Letting Go

"Mommy, I'm stuck." That's the way the adventure began. Three-year-old Crystal came to her mother holding in one hand her great grandmother's vase. The other hand couldn't be seen. It was stuck inside the vase.

Crystal's mother tried to move quickly without panicking, because the vase was valuable to her. Holding the vase and her little girl, she carried Crystal to the kitchen sink. She used warm soapy water to try to loosen the toddler's hand, which was indeed stuck. When soap didn't work, she reached for butter.

While greasing her child's wrist like a cake pan, she asked the obvious "mother question." "How in the world did you do this?" Crystal explained that she dropped candy down into the vase to see if she could still see it when it was at the very bottom. She couldn't. When she reached in for her candy, she couldn't get her hand back out.

The more time went on, the more serious the whole situation became. Mother called Grandmother to come over and help assess the situation. A neighbor suggested Vaseline. The apartment manager got the WD40. Still no luck. It seemed like the only way to get the child's hand out was to break the heirloom.

Grandma arrived with her calming presence and went over to Crystal, who was very upset and still very stuck. "Sweetheart," she said gently, "Mommy says you reached in the vase for candy. Is that right?"

"Mmm hmm," the child whimpered, still breathless from crying.

"Honey, tell Grandma the truth now. Do you still have hold of that candy?"

"Mmm hmm," she sobbed.

The grandmother patted her back to comfort her. "Let it go, child. Let it go."

The vase slipped off as smooth as silk.

(Rhonda VanDyke Colby, *Abingdon Women's Preaching Annual*, Series 2, Year B [Nashville: Abingdon Press, 1999], p. 62)

Reflection: Does this story make you smile? Can you imagine yourself as this child, stuck in an uncomfortable position just because you cannot let go of something you consider valuable? Could even this story present us with an image of sin?

Action: Give it a try with the vase on the table. Reach in for a piece of candy, and see if you can pull your hand out. Feel the resistance of the glass, and consider where you feel a similar resistance to change in your own life. Now, let go of the candy and slide your hand out. Reflect on what you might need to let loose in your life as you move toward God's forgiveness.

Release/Re-creation

In the day that the LORD God made the earth and the heavens, when no plant of the field was yet in the earth and no herb of the field had yet sprung up—for the LORD God had not caused it to rain upon the earth, and there was no one to till the ground; but a stream would rise from the earth, and water the whole face of the ground—then the LORD God formed [humanity] from the dust of the ground, and breathed into [their bodies] the breath of life; and [they] became [living beings]. And the LORD God planted a garden in Eden, in the east; and there he put [those] whom he had formed (Genesis 2:4b-8).

Reflection: As we exhale, our body expels stale air; as we inhale, our body takes in fresh air for our lungs. Think of exhaling as expelling the bad—the sin—and inhaling as receiving God's breath—the breath of creation—again. What can you let go? Just as your lungs can take in more air after a full exhalation, how much more of God's love and forgiveness can you inhale after releasing sin?

Action: Find a comfortable position. Close your eyes and concentrate on your breathing. Breathe slowly and fully from your diaphragm; when you do this, your stomach should expand outward and your chest should not rise significantly. You may want to offer your breath as a prayer—as you exhale, name something that you would like to let go, and as you inhale, say, "Thank you, God" for the forgiveness you can so readily receive.

Contaminated/Purified

But who can endure the day of his coming, and who can stand when he appears? For he is like a refiner's fire and like fullers' soap; he will sit as a refiner and purifier of silver, and he will purify the descendants of Levi and refine them like gold and silver, until they present offerings to the LORD in righteousness. (Malachi 3:2-3)

Reflection: Jewelers and scientists both know that one way to purify a material is with fire. All of the impurities burn away, and what is left is purified metal or a sterilized instrument. The process of confession and forgiveness can work in a similar fashion. What impurities mar your God-created beauty? You may think of a hurtful behavior, a distraction, an attitude, or addiction.

Action: Take a slip of paper from the table and write on it something that you consider to be an "impurity" in your life. Fold the paper, light the paper by the candle, and place it into the metal bowl. Please be careful, and do not hold onto the paper for too long.

Notice how quickly and easily the fire consumes the paper. So too, God easily purifies your soul through confession and forgiveness.

Built on Sand/Built on Rock

[Jesus said,] "Why do you call me 'Lord, Lord,' and do not do what I tell you? I will show you what someone is like who comes to me, hears my words, and acts on them. That one is like a man building a house, who dug deeply and laid the foundation on rock; when a flood arose, the river burst against that house but could not shake it, because it had been well built. But the one who hears and does not act is like a man who built a house on the ground without a foundation. When the river burst against it, immediately it fell, and great was the ruin of that house." (Luke 6:46-49)

Reflection: How do we know whether we are planted on bedrock or on sand? Jesus says the key question is whether our actions match our words. Perhaps a modern translation would be "where the rubber meets the road." When we are grounded, we can activate our faith. But if we are resting on something less than stable, we only skid and slip.

Action: Take a handful of sand from the bucket next to the table and let it run out of your hand, onto the table. Give this pile a name. Where are your words and your actions out of sync with God? Next, take a piece of rock from the other bucket, and place it on another part of the table. Call this rock the source of integrity in your life.

Consider how you can rest more of your life on the rock than on the sand. How might your faith become a firmer foundation in your life?

Futility/Fertility

[Jesus] began to teach them many things in parables, and in his teaching he said to them: "Listen! A sower went out to sow. And as he sowed, some seed fell on the path, and the birds came and ate it up. Other seed fell on rocky ground, where it did not have much soil, and it sprang up quickly, since it had no depth of soil. And when the sun rose, it was scorched; and since it had no root, it withered away. Other seed fell among thorns, and the thorns grew up and choked it, and it yielded no grain. Other seed fell into good soil and brought forth grain, growing up and increasing and yielding thirty and sixty and a hundredfold." And he said, "Let anyone with ears to hear listen!" (Mark 4:2-9)

Reflection: When Jesus explained the parable of the sower to his disciples, he told them that seed sown on good soil represented people who hear "the word of the kingdom" and understand it, and thus bear fruit in their lives. It is not always so. We miss so many opportunities for acting out our faith, often because we simply do not understand what God wants us to do.

Action: Plant a seed in a small peat pot in the basket in front of you. (You are welcome to bring it home, and be sure to water it when you do so!) As you put the seed into this good soil, pray that God will increase the fertile areas of your soul, and help you to clear out the rocks.

Casting Stones/Laying Our Stones Down

Early in the morning [Jesus] came again to the temple. All the people came to him and he sat down and began to teach them. The scribes and the Pharisees brought a woman who had been caught in adultery; and making her stand before all of them, they said to him, "Teacher, this woman was caught in the very act of committing adultery. Now in the law Moses commanded us to stone such women. Now what do you say?" They said this to test him, so that they might have some charge to bring against him. Jesus bent down and wrote with his finger on the ground. When they kept on questioning him, he straightened up and said to them, "Let anyone among you who is without sin be the first to throw a stone at her." (John 8:2-7)

Reflection: All of us carry around stones that we would like to hurl at others—stones of resentment, of regret, of anger and hurt, of pride. It is so much easier to condemn the sins of others than it is to examine our own lives.

Action: Take a handful of stones from the large bowl at the center of the table and hold onto them for a moment. Then, slowly release them, dropping them into one of the smaller bowls. Consider how much lighter your heart would be if you could release some of the judgments you make against others. What do you need to let go of, specifically?

You may wish to keep one stone—carry it in your pocket, perhaps—as a reminder to refrain from judging or accusing others in the coming weeks.

LAY LEADERS, FRONT AND CENTER

Introduction

In the church I (HKD) grew up in, lay people basically did two things in the worship service. We read the scripture lesson and we passed around the offering plates. During stewardship season someone would be asked to make a short speech about why she found her involvement in the church's life so very meaningful, but that was about it for personal testimony.

The main thing this pattern communicates is the clergyperson's profound distrust of the congregation. It implies that lay people can only be trusted with the simplest of tasks and those that it would be too awkward for the pastor to do herself.

Clearly, if our worship service is going to be grounded in high expectations for what God can do in the lives of every single person there, we need to give lay leaders a bigger role in worship. We need to communicate in everything we do that God can use anyone's words, anyone's ideas, anyone's body to be made known.

But old habits die hard. The worship leaders may be ready for lay leadership way before the lay leaders are ready. Remember, many people would rather do just about anything than speak in public. So you may not be giving laypeople the opportunity they've always dreamed of when you suggest that they give the sermon next week. Good lay leaders need more than an invitation. They need coaching and feedback and a chance to try again. But with care and support, they will grow in their confidence and in their faith, and your worship will never be the same.

Build Allies First

We are Congregationalists, not just by ordination, but by disposition. We believe in working together with the members of our congregation, not ruling over them. But we don't believe the first step to transforming worship is to form a worship committee or build a worship team. In fact, we believe that if we had started there, we'd never have the support for interactive worship that we do today.

Simply put, a lot of things we're proposing to do in worship work a lot better than most people think they will when they first hear about them. Start worship with the whole congregation yelling at a magus to wake up? Lead confession with a giant puppet on a backpack? Share a personal story with a total stranger during an interactive sermon? Imagine trying to sell those things to your average board of deacons. Yeah, right.

We don't start with committees—either those that already exist in our churches or new ones—because we don't want to give them the power to veto our experiments. Permanent worship changes, we understand, often do require the consent of our deacons, our council, or some other body. But we reserve the right to experiment—and to fail, and still experiment again. The methods described in this book will have significantly more support in your congregation if people have tried them out a few times and seen what a difference they make in their experience of worship.

But you cannot do it alone. You need to invite members of your congregation to experiment with you. Thus, almost everything in this book requires you to find volunteers, partners, and allies within the congregation. You need someone to wear the cow costume and someone to lead the congregation in a cheer. You need a whole crew to make puppets. You'll work with the deacons as you make changes in Communion, and you'll work with the choir as you make changes in music. If you start to stir all of these pots, good things will start to bubble up. But no single committee or group will be "in charge." As a result, worship will belong to the whole congregation. Everyone will be invested in the changes that are happening.

Build Worship Teams Second

The congregations we know that have creative, interactive worship week after week have built up teams of fully equipped lay leaders who are part of each week's worship planning from idea to implementation. Without a doubt, that's where we want to go. But getting there requires planning and patience. Until there is a critical mass of people in our congregations whose expectations for worship match our own, we are committed to working with others in more informal groups.

Expand the Job Description of Your Lay Leaders

One of the best ways to take a step toward building a worship team is to recruit and train a group of lay leaders who can really model for your congregation what it means to bring their whole selves before God in worship. In order for them to do that, you will have to rethink their description. You can expand your invitation to them without scaring everyone away from the job by taking it step by step.

Begin by simply expanding the number of things your lay leaders read. If they already read scripture, it's not much to ask them to lead the Call to Worship or the Prayer of Invocation or anything else that is already written out. Make a promise to yourself that you won't read anything that someone else could be reading.

Then, start having lay leaders give a brief introduction to your Prayer of Confession, and then allow them to be the one to give the Assurance of Pardon. Find resources that have creative and seasonal worship pieces from which your lay leaders could choose (many are available). Or, write your own, perhaps tying in a seasonal theme or an image from that morning's scripture.

As they expand the range of things they read out loud in worship, the lay leaders will get used to speaking more expressively, more personally, and more accessibly in worship. Following the Alcoholic's Anonymous slogan, "Fake it till you make it," your lay leaders will read other people's testimony until they can write their own.

Encourage Everyone to Pray

The "Pastoral Prayer" is one piece of the Sunday morning liturgy that it is particularly hard to get a layperson to lead. Even our most creative and adventurous lay leaders have balked at this one, so we've come up with other methods of inviting the congregation to participate. Now, the traditional "Pastoral Prayer" (you know the type—it follows the sermon and begins, "Lord, help us remember the three points I just made in my sermon. . . .") has lost all its appeal for us.

Many congregations invite members to share prayer concerns that will be included in the pastoral prayer. One easy shift is to ask for concerns and celebrations directly before the prayer, so that the tone of that time differs from that of the announcements period. Then, with some coaching and lots of encouragement, stop asking for prayer requests which you will then pray for, and instead invite everyone to simply pray their requests out loud during the pastoral prayer time.

You will find that some people will still "pray" by saying, "I'd like to ask for prayers for my Aunt Marge . . . ," but this is a huge step in the right direction.

Get Serious about Lay Leader Training

The fact of the matter is it's always easier to do scary things in groups of people who encourage us. And it's harder to shirk an assignment when everyone around you is doing it. So when you think you have a small group of lay leaders (even three or four) who have gotten comfortable reading creative pieces during worship, invite them to begin a process of "Lay Leader Training" with you.

This is no small request, so be sure to provide major incentives. Offer to begin with an overnight stay at a retreat house if you think that would be attractive. Offer high-quality child care. Provide a meal—a good one. Give each of them a devotional book—or a gift certificate to your nearest bookstore that carries Christian resources. Present them each with a special, engraved Bible. Don't think of this as bribery. You are showing them how seriously you take their role and how much they have to contribute to worship in your church.

Suggestions for a "curriculum" for a four-part lay worship leader training program follow this introduction.

Find Ways for Everyone to Share

Not everyone is going to become a lay leader, but everyone in your congregation has a story to share. We've tried to develop ways for even the shyest members of our congregation to share their stories, such as an annual Advent book. For details, see the examples that follow.

Lay Leader Training Curriculum

This four-part series is meant to extend over the course of a church year (September, January, March, and May, or whatever fits your church calendar). Each session is approximately an hour and a half in length. Thus, each can easily be held on a Saturday morning or a Sunday evening. With some additional time for discussion and personal study, each session could also become the basis for a short retreat.

Session One: What Does It Mean to Lead Worship?

Goals: (1) Engage lay leaders with the idea that they are more than readers—they are worship leaders. (2) Improve lay leaders' public speaking skills—volume and quality of voice, eye contact, and body language.

Ice breaker: Talk about your worst public speaking fantasy—or experience! Have you ever had a dream that you were giving a speech naked? Have you ever forgotten your lines while on stage? Be sure to have a story of your own ready to share. The goal here is to dispel anxiety by saying out loud what our worst fears are—and then laughing at those fears together.

Pep Talk: Throughout the training, it is extremely important for you, the worship leader, to speak personally, passionately, and positively about worship. Talk to them about what being a worship leader means to you. Share a story of a time when you felt worship really worked well. Describe what being a part of good worship feels like to you, and how it changes you inside and out. Make sure every single person in the room knows that worship leadership is important and valuable.

Exercise: Using a well-known Bible passage, a standard Call to Worship, or other piece with which your lay leaders would be familiar, experiment with reading out loud. Try reading really loudly. Try reading it as if it were extremely urgent and important. Try reading with exaggerated expressiveness—go ahead and get goofy about it! And then, read the piece "for real" while still trying to communicate effectively with voice, face, and body.

If you have access to video equipment, it can be of great use here. You might either review videos you have made of each lay leader during past worship services, or tape each leader during your workshop. Play the tapes, and invite comments from the group. Be sure to give a structure for the feedback, encouraging listeners to comment on something they liked, as well as something they thought could be improved.

Session Two:
Noticing the Words We Use in Worship

Goal: To connect our lay leaders with the words they are saying, sensitizing them to the kinds of words that work well in worship.

Ice Breaker: This week, you might want to start off by playing with words a bit. For example, play "Fictionary" by choosing a word out of a dictionary that no one knows, and invite each person to write a creative definition of the word. Mix the fake definitions up with the real one, and see if anyone can guess what the word really means.

Pep Talk: Reinforce with your lay leaders how important their job is. Talk about moments since the last training when you thought worship went well. Compliment the lay leaders on their work in particular, and tell any stories you might have about ways in which their leadership aided the congregation's experience of worship.

Exercise: Distribute the handouts with lots of different Calls to Worship, Prayers of Invocation, Calls to Confession, Assurances of Pardon, Invitations to the Offering, or any other worship element that you or the lay leaders read in worship. Have each person scan through the readings, circling words that jump out at them—ones that are particularly vivid or pleasing or thought-provoking.

When everyone has had a chance to do this, ask them to call out the words they circled and write them on a piece of newsprint. Discuss the list as a group.

- Did we circle many of the same words, or different ones?
- Are there any similarities among the words we picked?
- What words did we by and large leave out?
- What similar words could we add to this list?
- What effect does the language we choose have on our experience of worship?

Then, invite your group to begin to write their own worship pieces using some of the words on your newsprint list. Pass out pieces of paper and pens and give everyone five or ten minutes. There is nothing like a little peer pressure—and peer support—to get people writing.

Take turns reading the pieces out loud. Encourage everyone to give their feedback to the reader, both compliments and suggestions for improvement.

Encourage everyone to use one of the pieces they've written in worship in the coming months.

Session Three:
Writing Our Own Creative Pieces

Goal: To invite lay leaders to create original worship pieces using vivid images and language.

Ice Breaker: Play "Mad Libs" with a standard Call to Worship or other piece your lay leaders read. Transcribe the piece onto newsprint, leaving out key nouns, verbs, or adjectives. Keep the newsprint out of sight and ask your lay leaders to supply the most wild and vivid words they can think of for each category. Fill the blanks in the worship piece using the words they provide, and have a good laugh!

Pep Talk: Spend some time complimenting your lay leaders on the work they have done so far, and the gift they are giving to the congregation. Encourage the group to debrief their work since they last met. What do they think has been working, and what hasn't worked? Do they have feedback for each other, or for you? Take time to hear it, and honor them as your partners in making worship effective for your congregation.

Exercise: Divide the group into pairs or triads and ask them to complete the following sentences in as many ways as possible:

- Worship is like a_____.
- Good worship is as _____ as a _____.
- Confession is like a _____.
- God's forgiveness is as _____ as a _____.

Make up a few more of your own!

After ten minutes or so, pull the group back together, and have each group read their answers out loud. Make notes of the metaphors and images they use on newsprint where everyone can see.

When everyone has debriefed, invite everyone to write a piece for worship (Words of Welcome, Call to Confession, Assurance of Pardon, or some other element), expanding on one of the images or metaphors that either they, or someone else in the group, suggested. Allow some time for writing, and then invite everyone to read theirs out loud. Encourage positive feedback as well as suggestions for improvement. Just to be fun, you might want to offer one that's a bit silly. (Worship is like a watermelon? Confession is like a really big sneeze when you have a bad cold? You get the idea.)

Session Four: Getting Personal

Goal: To invite lay leaders to compose original worship pieces that include personal stories.

Ice Breaker: Since people may be anxious about the idea of getting personal with confessions, why not make a game out of this to start off? Play "Two Lies and a Truth." Encourage everyone to write down three "confessions," only one of which is true. The more outrageous the better! Take turns reading them out loud and guessing which one is true.

Pep Talk: Here's your chance to model the power of personal story. Tell the group, as simply and directly as you can, a story about confession and forgiveness, or a story about coming into worship, or a story about prayer (or all of the above).

Then, share with the group some examples of pieces written by lay leaders that use personal stories as part of their worship leadership. Here are two examples to get you started:

> As most of you know, Vin and I are newlyweds. There was a lot to get used to, especially in the very beginning. Vin and I are alike in many ways, but one way we are very different is in our eating habits. I'm a picky eater; Vin will eat anything. I pick my food up daintily with my fork; Vin sometimes uses a fork, but often finds that a piece of bread or his fingers will work just as well. I eat my food one thing at a time; Vin mixes it all up in a glorious mess in the middle of his plate.
>
> You are probably wondering what eating habits have to do with confessing our sins to God. I remember one of our first dinners together as a married couple. I also eat more quickly than Vin and was done long before he was. I was antsy. There were chores and homework to be done. We hadn't said much to each other all through dinner. I just wanted to escape the table and get on with things. However, I forced myself to stay until Vin was done eating. The antsiness continued, but after a while one of us said something, the other responded, and before long we were having a deep, intense discussion. I don't remember what it was about, but I do remember clearly the strong sense of closeness I felt when it was over. It had happened because we both had been willing to be at the table with each other. So it is with God when we confess. It doesn't always matter so much what we say, but it does matter that we are here, willing to do it. In this way we remain in relationship with God. Be assured that God is always there at the table too, ready to forgive, and eager to enter into a still closer relationship with us. (Sara Folta)

Some of you met my parents when they came to visit a few years ago. My mother made a big impression, partly because she spoke to the Odds & Ends club, but mostly because she's outgoing, dynamic, and a storyteller. My father, on the other hand, is content to remain in the background. People frequently ask me about my mother—no one asks me about my father.

As we prepare ourselves for prayer, I'd like to ask us to give a thought to people in our lives who don't say much, the people who are always there, and who are content to be reliable and undemanding. We are a people of opportunity. If we have neglected good people in the past, we have yet the opportunity to remember and acknowledge them. If we have erred, we can yet mend our ways. And we do so, knowing that God has forgiven our neglect, forgives our errors, and will forgive us again. (John Olson)

Exercise: There's nothing to it but to do it. After reading examples of this kind of worship piece, give paper and pens to everyone and send them off somewhere by themselves to write a story. Be sure to give them several options to choose from, and specific questions they might consider to get their ideas flowing. For example:

Welcome to Worship: What does worship mean to you? Why do you bother to get out of bed and come on Sunday? What makes you feel welcome when you are new somewhere?

Call to Confession: What does confession mean to you? Have you had an experience which put the experience in a new light? Can you tell about a time when you had to apologize, or repair something, or make something right, or do something over again?

Assurance of Pardon: If you could say one or two sentences to someone who wasn't sure that he or she was loved and accepted by God, what would you say? Is there a story you could tell him or her?

After time is up, invite everyone back to read their pieces (even if they aren't quite finished) and to respond to those others have written. Give lots and lots of affirmation, and be sure to make copies of what everyone has written before they go. Invite every lay leader to revise and polish their pieces for use in worship.

Lay Leader Training Frequently Asked Questions

Is there an open invitation for the training?

We believe that everyone can play a part in worship, and that some people have particular gifts for particular areas of leadership. So, when you are recruiting for the lay worship leader training, make sure to seek out those people you think are gifted for such leadership. Affirm their innate abilities and personally invite them to join you in the training.

That said, make sure that the invitation to the training is extended to all in the church by publicizing the training in your newsletter and in the weekly bulletin. By opening the training to all people, you may have to deal with a few difficult people but you may also be pleasantly surprised by the hidden gifts for worship leadership that you discover in people you had overlooked.

Now that we have people who are specifically equipped for the task, can just anyone lead worship?

We know of churches that have answered this question in many different ways and have found a balance that is right for them. We do suggest that you find meaningful ways for anyone, regardless of age, background, or training, to participate in worship, but that doesn't mean that everything has to be open to everyone.

Here are a few suggestions to make sure that your whole congregation really is involved in worship leadership:

1. **Have some roles that are for everyone.** Make reading scripture, reading the Call to Worship, or leading the Offering open to anyone who wishes to participate. In fact, seek out and invite people who might not think to volunteer (teens, disabled folks, mothers of babies, etc.). That way, anyone, regardless of training, age, or ability, has a meaningful way to publicly lead worship.
2. **Work in pairs.** Consider teaming up people who have been trained to lead worship and those who have not, and divide up the lay leadership tasks based on each person's training and abilities.

3. **Elevate other ways in which people serve in worship.** We rarely recognize less "public" ways of leading in worship, such as singing in the choir, greeting people at the door of the sanctuary, making sure that the tablecloths are clean and pressed for Communion, baking Communion bread, or designing worship banners and other art in the worship space. These jobs can truly be thankless. When we take the time to thank people ritually in worship for the less public ways in which they lead in worship, we celebrate the rich variety of gifts of the Spirit. Public worship leadership then is not the only way that people know that they matter to the community and to God.

OUT OF THE POOL AND INTO THE OCEAN

A number of years ago, when my twin sons, Paul and Isaac, were a little over two years old, I (HKD) tried to introduce them to the joy of swimming. I put a lot of effort into my plan. I signed up for a "Mommy and Me" swim class at our local Y and even hired a babysitter to come with me each week so that each child would have an adult with whom to swim, as was the requirement of the class. I got swim diapers and swimsuits and little goggles, and read stories about swimming to the boys in anticipation. They seemed wary, but I figured any apprehension would soon abate, and in no time they would joyfully anticipate every trip to the pool.

It was not to be. At the first class they actually got into the water for a few minutes, but from then on, they wouldn't even do that. They would scream and struggle and cling to the legs of the bench by the pool. After a couple of weeks of this, it became impossible even to get their swimsuits on. One week, after chasing them both around the locker room for the entire forty-five-minute class period, I threw a shoe in frustration and narrowly missed one of their heads. I realized I had to admit defeat. My twins did not like the water. They did not like to swim. And no amount of scheming or cajoling or bribing or threatening was going to change that fact.

That summer, when we vacationed with my husband's family for a week at a cottage on a lake, I told everyone up front—the twins don't like the water. Don't try to take them swimming because they hate it. We took turns hanging out with them on shore, playing in the sand with dump trucks and buckets and shovels while everyone else enjoyed the water.

Their cousin Anna, just eight months older, could spend the entire day in the lake. She pretended she was a fish, she found treasures in the sandy bottom, she begged every adult for rides and spins, and she dumped buckets of water over her head and laughed and laughed.

Paul and Isaac watched her with interest. Then one day, a ball rolled into the lake, and Paul ran to catch it. He splashed into the water and then out again before he really noticed what he was doing. Then Isaac threw the ball in again. Laughing, Paul ran to get it again. "Again! Again!" Anna yelled, and this time, Isaac threw the ball a little farther in. Paul followed, with Isaac at his heels, and before they knew it, they were up to their armpits in the lake, laughing and splashing with their cousin. They spent most of the afternoon in there, and they've enjoyed the water ever since.

Little three-year-old Anna did something that the swimming instructor, my babysitter, and I didn't do—she showed my kids how much fun it is to play in water. By simply having a lot of fun in the lake, she invited them to do something that was new and scary to them. They responded to her delight—and when they did, it felt like it was their idea all along.

Early on in my ministry, an older parishioner said to me on her way out the door on a Sunday morning, "It sure looks like you're having fun up there!" I wasn't sure how to take the comment. Did it seem like I was goofing off? Did I lack the proper *gravitas* of an older minister? Was my pleasure in worship a bit unseemly? But remembering my twins in the lake, I decided to take the comment as a sincere compliment—and as the starting point for an invitation to a more responsive, interactive, and transformative experience of worship.

The bottom line is, if we ever hope to invite people to splash and frolic in God's holy, saving, thirst-quenching water, we have to jump in first.

So go ahead. Do front flips and back dives. Blow bubbles. Try out somersaults, cartwheels, and walking on your hands. Open your eyes underwater and notice what is down there. Bring up any treasures you find so that everyone can experience them. Climb up to the top of the high diving board, the one that makes you dizzy when you look down from it, take a deep breath, and jump. And when the dive you thought was going to be graceful turns out to be a painful belly flop, make sure you acknowledge the pain, find out if there is someone who can teach you what you don't know, pray plenty, and climb up and try again. And whatever you do, don't stop inviting other people into the water to join you.

No doubt about it, it is safer to stand at the edge, standing dry and protected, keeping our distance. It has not always been easy for us to take risks to make worship more creative, interactive, and dynamic. Like everyone else, we are sensitive to criticism and we don't like it when people we care about are mad at us. I can still feel the sting of the comment, "What is that [expletive deleted] thing doing in here! We're going to trip over that!" when a certain parishioner saw the All Saints' Day river of fabric in our sanctuary. It was all I could do not to burst into tears, grab my fabric, and enroll in dental hygienist school.

We have just two more pieces of advice for those times when you want to get out, dry off, and never return to worship again. First, find a friend to support you. Better yet, find a friend who wants to try some new things in worship too, and make a plan to support each other. Agree to try out new things on the same Sunday and then compare notes. Pray for each other daily. Email often, especially after Sunday worship. After you've tried out some of the resources in this book, get together for a day-long retreat—we recommend a place with wireless internet access, lots of tea, and, if you can swing it, a hot tub—and write your own pieces.

It's no accident that two people wrote this book. We couldn't have done many of the things in this book without one another. Sure, two heads are better than one, and our writing and creative ideas are always enhanced by a conversation together. But two hearts are also better than one. We have supported and cheered one another on even when it seemed that the risks we were taking in worship were too risky.

I (NWL) remember distinctly the process of working on the puppets together (**Changed and Challenged by Jesus**). After the initial excitement of planning and praying about making the stories in the Gospel of John come alive, I quickly had second thoughts. What was I thinking, I wondered, expecting my congregation of folks from rural New Hampshire to welcome eight-foot parade puppets into their sanctuary? But the fact that I had an ally in this process made it possible for me to say to my congregation, "We are going to do this exciting new thing together. And you are going to love it!" And love it they did.

Second, and most important, remember that God is the center of worship. In fact, God is the center of everything. While it is you who has the privilege of coming up with fun, floaty toys to play with and creative new ways to swim, it is God who made the water. Never forget that. Keep praying for clarity and humility and the receptivity to see that God is going to show up and be present in your worship—and your life—in ways you cannot even begin to dream up on your own.

Several years ago, we crafted worship around the story in Acts 16 when Paul meets Lydia. The text is very clear that Lydia is "outside the gates" and it is there that Paul finds her and tells her of Jesus' radically inclusive love. During the sermon time, I (NWL) told the congregation my most left-out moment from junior high. People laughed and commiserated since who didn't, at age thirteen, feel completely left out from time to time? After telling them my story, I invited the members of the congregation to pair up and to describe to one another a time when they had been left out. I told them that I knew that they were taking a risk and I was proud of them for that. I also emphasized that this worship service was not to be someone's future "left out" story and, if someone couldn't find a partner he or she should let me know.

People quickly found partners and started sharing their stories. I circulated around the sanctuary and saw an older parishioner I knew well sitting by himself and not talking to anyone. I went over to him and asked if he had ever experienced being left out. "My whole life" was his reply. I asked him about that and he told me that his parents had put him in an orphanage when he was four. He had remained there his whole childhood, outside the gates of family and home. Despite having a healthy, warm relationship with him, I had never heard that story before. I said to him, "I never knew that." He replied, "Most people don't."

I had known this man for more than a year and a half, and every Sunday morning I made a point of coming over to him before worship and checking in. Through pastoral visits and casual conversations, I knew much about the last sixty years of his life—his wife and family, his involvement with the church, his commitment to the Masons, and the work he had done for most of his life. This person was no stranger to me. How is it that we had that conversation in worship?

It was the power of being in worship with others who were taking risks and being vulnerable that allowed the man to share his heartbreakingly painful story. We didn't make God do something. We didn't try to create an artificial "experience" of God, designed for our own entertainment. We simply began with an expectation that God would be powerfully present in our worship and that we would be open to God's transforming grace. We raised our confidence levels and believed that we could support one another in diving deeper into the life of the Spirit. We laughed and cried. That was all. God did the work of bringing the power of wholeness and complete love into that man's life. But we did our small part.

After such experiences, and we know that you will have them, you'll never want to go back—everything else will just feel like marking time in the kiddie pool. "Come on in," Jesus calls. "The water is fabulous!"